HOW THE EBOOKS WORK

The eBooks are provided in EPUB file format. Please note that you will need an eBook reader installed on your device to open the file. Many devices come with this as standard, but you may still need to install one manually from Google Play.

The eBook content is identical to the content in the printed guide.

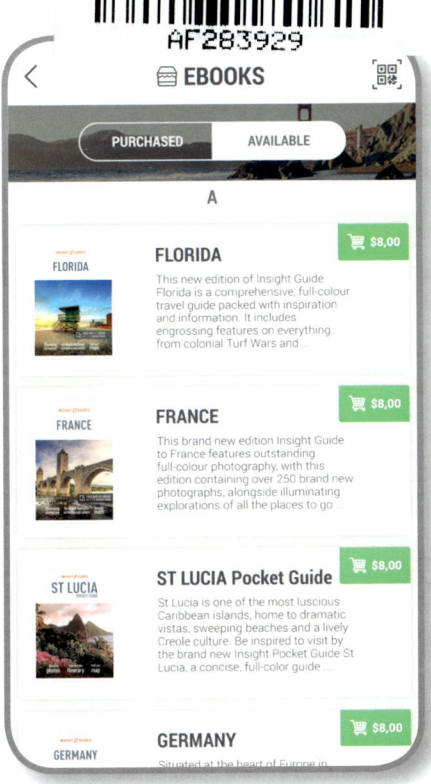

HOW TO DOWNLOAD THE WALKING EYE APP

1. Download the Walking Eye App from the App Store or Google Play.
2. Open the app and select the scanning function from the main menu.
3. Scan the QR code on this page – you will then be asked a security question to verify ownership of the book.
4. Once this has been verified, you will see your eBook in the purchased ebook section, where you will be able to download it.

Other destination apps and eBooks are available for purchase separately or are free with the purchase of the Insight Guide book.

CONTENTS

ANCIENT WONDERS

Route 6 visits the archaeological sites of Pompeii and Herculaneum, while a trip to the Campi Flegrei (route 5) takes in sights from a Roman amphitheatre to the mysterious cave of the Cumaean sibyl.

RECOMMENDED ROUTES FOR...

ART BUFFS

Naples' central churches (route 1) are full of Baroque masterpieces, and the modern art museum is an essential stop. Don't miss the Museo di Capodimonte (route 4), one of Italy's finest art museums.

ESCAPING THE CROWDS

Despite its astonishing sights, the Campi Flegrei area (route 5) is low on tourists; Capri (route 10) is heaving during the day, but at night is free of crowds; and Procida (route 12) is a sleepy refuge from the bay's busier sights.

FAMILIES

In Naples, the kid-friendly combination of castle, park and aquarium make route 3 ideal, while the friendly atmosphere of Sorrento (route 7) and the lovely beaches of Ischia (route 11) make these a good bet for families.

FOODIES

For genuine Neapolitan pizza, the rowdy *centro storico* (route 1) is the place, and a fish feast in Borgo Marinaro (route 2) is a must. The Sorrentine Peninsula (route 7) has a clutch of gourmet restaurants.

BACK TO NATURE

The Sorrentine Peninsula (route 7) is a walker's paradise, while Ischia (route 11) offers natural hot springs, and Capri (route 10) has wonderful walks. For an encounter with Mother Nature, visit Vesuvius (route 6).

SEASIDE FUN

Positano's beaches (route 8) are large, with plenty of facilities; the Sorrentine Peninsula (route 7) has good, tucked-away swimming spots, while Ischia and Procida (routes 11 and 12) boast lovely beaches and crystal-clear water.

STREET LIFE

For a dose of the street life that defines the city, a stroll through Naples' *centro storico* (route 1) can't be beaten. Sorrento (route 7) and Capri (route 10) are also always bustling, too, if more genteel.

INTRODUCTION

An introduction to Naples's geography, customs and culture, plus illuminating background information on cuisine, history and what to do when you're there.

A patriotic young cyclist

EXPLORE NAPLES

Disorderly, rowdy, exhilarating – the capital of the Italian South is like nowhere else. The Bay of Naples holds its own charms, from dazzling islands to slumbering volcanoes, world–class archaeological sites and the sinuous Amalfi Coast.

Naples lives by its own rules. Utterly lacking in tourist-ready gloss, the city demands that visitors give in to the flow of local life; the noise and chaos may be somewhat alarming at first, but a wander through the *centro storico* will very soon win you over.

All of human life is played out here: boys dodge the traffic to play street football; old men cluster on street corners and argue about politics; mopeds bearing entire families buzz down the narrow streets, klaxons blaring; workers cram into tiny bars, putting the world to rights in their coffee break.

And those clichés of a bygone, earthier Italy that have all but disappeared elsewhere – glittering shrines, lines of washing and raucous local markets – are everywhere you look in Naples.

It is the third-largest city in Italy after Rome and Milan, with around 978,000 inhabitants. When its crowded and ever-expanding suburbs are included, however, the figure is around 4.5 times bigger than this.

At the heart of it all, and visible for miles around, stands Vesuvius, a potent symbol of the beauty and cruelty of nature and a huge influence on the Neapolitan character.

Beyond Naples' suburbs, nature takes over. Seek refuge from the clamorous city along the Amalfi Coast, in the rugged Sorrentine Peninsula and on the islands. There's something for everyone here, whether you're looking for a family break, a romantic getaway or a few days of solo pampering.

GEOGRAPHY AND LAYOUT

The Bay of Naples and Amalfi Coast are part of Campania, one of the four provinces that make up southern Italy. The landscape is volcanic, its topography formed by ancient craters and the deposits left by thousands of years of volcanic activity.

The most prominent landmark on the bay is Vesuvius (1,017m/3,336ft), dormant since its last eruption in 1944. The only active crater in the region today is the Solfatara, which, according to scientists' latest warnings, is approaching a 'critical state' that could cause a large eruption.

The southern end of the bay is bounded by the Monti Lattari, a hill

The Galleria Umberto I

Outside Caffè Gambrinus

range that forms the backbone of the Amalfi Coast.

Naples

Once you get your bearings, Naples is an easy city to navigate, and the main areas of interest to tourists can all be covered on foot. Driving is not a viable option – traffic is solid in the city centre, parking nightmarish and Neapolitan drivers anarchic, to say the least. To travel between city districts, stick to the cheap and easy public-transport system. Buses can be slow, and the metro is undergoing a major overhaul, but the funiculars that ferry people up and down the Vomero hill are ultra-efficient, and the trains and boats in and out of the city are plentiful and smooth running.

Day trips from Naples

Naples is a good base for exploring the historic sites in the bay area: trains to the Campi Flegrei, Pompeii and Herculaneum run frequently from the train station at Piazza Garibaldi. Try to arrive as early as you can at these busy sites, especially during the summer months, when they can be very crowded.

The bay area as far as Castellammare di Stabia is built-up, with ugly industrial estates and housing blocks at various stages of disrepair, but between the grim buildings sprout citrus trees and olive groves, and the sea and mountainous backdrop are constantly magnificent. South of Castellammare, the urban sprawl dwindles away, replaced by a captivating landscape of green hills, plunging cliffs and picture-postcard towns.

Beyond Naples

After a few days exploring the city, you will be craving some calm. The laid-back town of Sorrento is perfectly positioned for exploring the islands, the Amalfi Coast and Pompeii. If you don't want to hire a car and tackle the Amalfi drive yourself, the blue SITA buses run regular services between Sorrento, Positano and Amalfi.

Superstitious Naples

Naples seems to have spent its entire history waiting for Vesuvius to erupt, which goes some way towards explaining the local character traits of seize-the-day exuberance and a deep-seated reliance on superstitions to ward off harm. The superstitions that are part of everyday life are fascinating to outsiders: three times a year, the city holds its breath to see whether the Miracle of San Gennaro will keep its citizens safe; the elaborate shrines dotted throughout the city are eloquent and touching testimonies to the faith of the populace; La Smorfia – an archaic dream dictionary – is widely used by locals to interpret their dreams and divine the winning lottery numbers; and the *corno* – a horn-shaped lucky charm supposed to ward off the evil eye – is possibly Naples' most popular souvenir.

In summer, ferries carry day-trippers from Sorrento and Naples to the islands. But to absorb properly the wild beauty of Capri's coastline and find time to relax in Ischia's hot springs after sightseeing, consider an overnight stay. Procida is so small that you could easily walk round it in a day, though it is still a pretty, peaceful place to spend the night, and only a short hop from Naples.

HISTORY

For nearly three thousand years, Naples was fought over and occupied by a succession of foreign powers. Greeks, Romans, Normans, Arabs, Angevins, Spanish and Bourbons – all left their mark, not just on the streets and buildings, but on the language, culture and character of the Neapolitans themselves. Gregarious by nature, their clan-based communities and innate disrespect for authority are rooted in centuries of foreign domination.

Art and architecture

Naples' chequered history has resulted in a variety of architectural styles, though medieval, Renaissance and Baroque churches, castles and *palazzi* predominate. Much of the art you are likely to see in Naples is in the Baroque style. This was sparked by Caravaggio, who pitched up here in 1606 after the Roman authorities put a price on his head for killing his opponent in a tennis match. A wanted man, he didn't stick around for long, but long enough to paint some of his greatest paintings and influence a new generation of artists with the revolutionary realism of his paintings. The works of his followers decorate churches and *palazzi* throughout the city.

Post-war Naples

For an insight into how Naples' recent history has shaped the city, read Norman Lewis's fascinating *Naples '44*, a no-holds memoir of the Allied occupation during World War II, when the city was stripped to its bare bones. The day-to-day dealings of the people are told as a series of humorous, tragic and astonishing anecdotes that help to shed light on some of the more eccentric characteristics of its present-day citizens.

CLIMATE

Spring and autumn are by far the best seasons for visiting the Bay of Naples. The weather from April to June and September to October is not too hot for sightseeing but still warm enough to swim. July and August can be unpleasantly hot and humid, especially in the city (hence the August exodus, when most shops and restaurants close). These two months are also peak season, when the islands and coastal resorts swarm with tourists. Winters are generally mild, though unless the ghostly, abandoned atmosphere of resorts off-season appeals, the coastal areas are less inviting. Bathing facilities close in early October and many

The sprawling, semi-circular Piazza Plebiscito

restaurants and hotels close between November and Easter.

PEOPLE AND CUSTOMS

Like the rest of the Italian south, the pace of life here is unhurried, and the easy-going locals place importance on the simple things in life – mainly good food and good company. As a generalisation, Neapolitans (like all Italians) seem to be united in their belief in the importance of the family. This can be seen in the reluctance of young people to leave home until they get married – although financial concerns, especially high rents,

---

DON'T LEAVE NAPLES WITHOUT...

Trying the local tipple. *Limoncello* – the sticky, sweet local liqueur – is everywhere you look in these parts (and especially in Sorrento, see page 62). Most restaurants will serve you a shot of it at the end of your meal, or you can taste it in one of the dedicated shops in town. Sorrento's Limonoro (Via San Cesareo 49–53; tel: 081-878 5348) also sells *limoncello* sweets and chocolates; even the local *scialatielli* pasta is lemon-scented.

Listening out for Neapolitan music. Wander down any central backstreet and you're almost bound to hear Musica Napoletana being warbled through an open window. The *canzone napoletana* became a formally recognised genre in the 1830s, thanks to the Festival of Piedigrotta, a local songwriting competition. It petered out in the 1950s, but classics such as *Funiculì, Funiculà* and *O Sole Mio* remain as popular as ever. See also page 22.

Grabbing a gelato. If you are in need of a cool down, pick up an ice cream at Gay Odin (see page 36), Chalet Ciro (see page 45) or Fantasia Gelati (points across the city, including Via Toledo 381; www.fanta siagelati.it), some of the city's best gelaterie. If you really want to fit in, do as the locals do and have one during the customary evening *passeggiata*, or promenade.

Eating a pizza. The city is the birthplace of pizza, with the authentic Neapolitan variety having a thin crust and being cooked quickly in a wood-fired oven. Di Matteo (see page 36) is a good place to try it.

Spire-spotting. Keep an eye out for the soaring guglie (marble spires) that embellish three of the old town's squares visited on route 1, see page 30. The first, dedicated to the Virgin, stands outside the Gesù Nuovo church; the second, on Piazza San Domenico, gave thanks for the end of the plague epidemic; the third, in Piazza Sisto Riario Sforza, was erected in honour of San Gennaro, Naples' patron saint, when the city escaped unscathed after Vesuvius erupted in 1631.

Eating for free. Partake of the fine Italian tradition of the *aperitivo*. Head into a wine bar around 6pm and you'll probably find an array of bar snacks laid out for free. In some places, you can eat so much that you may not have room for dinner. See page 19.

Church interior

also have a lot to do with this, as does the fact that many young men, in particular, rely on a doting mother to do their washing and cooking. This is known as *mammismo*, the cult of the mother, but as more and more Italian women now have careers, this may be the last generation that will benefit from such long-term nurturing. The importance of the family can also be seen in the fact that

TOP TIPS FOR EXPLORING NAPLES AND THE AMALFI COAST

Antiques market. During the Fiera Antiquaria Napoletana (www.fieraantiquarianapoletana.it), antiques sellers set up their wares between the Villa Comunale and Via Caracciolo on the waterfront, selling anything from old armoires to Christmas crib figurines. The market takes place on the third Sunday of the month and the preceding Saturday (except Aug), and the fourth Sunday of the month and preceding Saturday (except Jun–Aug), from 8am to 2pm.

Budget opera. If you're aged under 30, on a budget and fancy a night out at the opera, you're in luck in Naples. Discounted tickets to world-class performances at the Teatro San Carlo are available to under-30s for around €20.

Sightseeing shuttle. A shuttle bus service run by City Sightseeing (www.napoli.city-sightseeing.it) starts in Piazza Treiste e Trento and runs to the Museo di Capodimonte every hour from 9.15am to 5.15pm, taking in the Museo Archeologico en route.. Tickets are €7 (see page 106).

Reaching the coast. If the Amalfi Coast is your main destination and you're on a budget, consider breaking your journey from the airport with a night in Sorrento, as there is no direct transport from the airport to the coast and the trip involves a number of buses and several hours.

Guided walks. Giovanni Visetti (tel: 339-694 2911; www.giovis.com) is an experienced walking guide with a wealth of knowledge on trails all over the coast. Giovanni also runs a walking club – experienced hikers are welcome to join the walks for free. Alternatively, check out the free guided walks at www.hikingcampania.com.

A cheap eat. Eating out in Capri can eat into your budget. Da Brioches, an excellent *alimentari* at 5 Via Fuorlovado in Capri Town (daily 8am–8.30pm), will make you up a panino for a few euros and sells plenty of tasty treats for a picnic.

Budget pampering. If your budget won't quite stretch to a spa, head to the little bay of Sorgeto, near Forio, accessible by sea or down a long flight of steps, where hot mineral springs and fumeroles bubble up under the sea, even in the depths of winter. It's also worth knowing that you can get into the Giardini Poseidon Park an hour before closing for around €5 (the day rate is €32).

Diving off Procida. The island's limpid blue waters are perfect for diving. Procida Diving Centre (tel: 081-896 8385; www.vacanzeprocida.it) organises dives from €45, with instructor and equipment.

Tomatoes and mozzarella　　　　　　　*Limoncello, a favourite tipple*

ria) or ice-cream parlour *(gelateria)*. Savoury snacks and cakes are usually eaten standing up or on the hoof. However, in summer there are plenty of pavement cafés with outdoor seating where you can nurse a drink, chat and people-watch for as long as you like.

Meals

Restaurant meals are eaten in either a *ristorante* or the traditionally simpler *trattoria* or *osteria* – though the distinction is somewhat blurred these days. Many restaurants serve pizza too, but pizzerias generally offer only pizza; a pizza *al taglio* is usually a hole-in-the-wall pizzeria selling slices to take away. A *tavola calda* is a cheap self-service place, offering hot and cold dishes.

DRINKS

The wines of the Italian south are enjoying a renaissance, and Campania produces some excellent varieties, benefiting from an abundance of indigenous grapes and a favourable climate. The best of the local wines, such as Fiano and Falanghina, derive from ancient varieties introduced by the Greeks and Romans, and may well be the forebears of the more renowned Cabernet and Chardonnay. Greco di Tufo is a dry white, ideal with fish dishes or soups, while Falanghina and Fiano di Avellino are fruity yet dry.

Ischia produces good local whites, notably Biancolella, cultivated on the steep slopes of Monte Epomeo.

Among the reds, the *aglianico* grape reigns supreme; Italy's longest-cultivated variety, it is thought to have been introduced to Campania by the Greeks in around 750 BC. Nowadays, the grape goes into making the highly prized, full-bodied Taurasi.

Dinner is preceded by *aperitivi* – traditionally Prosecco – and followed by *digestivi* such as *grappa*, the Italian firewater. For those with a sweeter tooth, there is *limoncello*, a strong but sweet lemon liqueur.

The morning coffee is usually knocked back at the counter rather than lingered over (and you'll be charged around double for the privilege of sitting down). Italians everywhere like to end a meal with a caffè, and the Neapolitan espresso is hailed as the best in the country, served very hot and very strong; if you like it weaker, ask for a macchiato (with a drop of hot milk).

Food and Drink prices

Throughout this book, price ranges for a two-course meal for one with a glass of house wine are as follows:
€€€€ = Over €40
€€€ = €26–40
€€ = €16–25
€ = Under €15

Local pottery

SHOPPING

Naples and the Amalfi Coast may not compete with Rome and Milan in terms of designer shopping, but a wealth of independent boutiques, traditional crafts and lively neighbourhood markets keep diehard shoppers amused.

Naples' main attraction for shoppers lies in the individuality of its boutiques and specialist shops, and the atmosphere of its shopping streets. To shop as the locals do, take it slowly, punctuating your window-shopping with plenty of breaks for *gelato* and coffee.

NAPLES

Whatever you buy, take home a local speciality to remind you of your trip: a bottle of *limoncello*, some spicy salami, a set of Christmas crib figurines or a pair of made-to-measure sandals.

Designer fashion

Most up-market designer shops are in Chiaia. Via dei Mille and Via dei Filangeri, and their side streets, are crammed with boutiques selling clothes, shoes, leather, jewellery and soft furnishings. Big-name designers – Ferragamo, Armani, Versace, Gucci, et al – cluster around Piazza dei Martiri and Via Calabritto. Finely crafted bags, belts and leather goods can be found at **Tramontano** (Via Chiaia 143) while **Marinella**'s legendary ties are worn by royalty and film stars (Riviera di Chiaia 287).

Mainstream fashion

More affordable fashions can be found on Via Toledo at chains such as Benetton and Stefanel. The street is lined with pavement hawkers selling imitations of designer handbags, scarves, watches, sunglasses and jewellery; haggling is expected. The Galleria Umberto I, an elegant 19th-century shopping arcade, is a retreat from the heat. Vomero is home to the department store **Coin** (Via Scarlatti 90–98; www.coin.it), while Chiaia has the cheaper **Upim** (17 Via Nicola Nisco; www.upim.it).

Arts and crafts

The *centro storico*, particularly along and around Spaccanapoli, is filled with artisans' workshops, jewellers, grocery stores and specialist shops. You will often find an entire street dedicated to one particular product: Via San Sebastiano has back-to-back music shops; Via Santa Maria di Costantinopoli is good for antiques. A good place for a Neapolitan souvenir is Via di San Gregorio Armeno, full of stalls selling terracotta figures and kitsch paraphernalia for the decoration of Christmas cribs *(presepi)*, alongside *smorfia* boards (a kind of dream-inter-

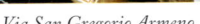
Via San Gregorio Armeno

Cameos are popular in Naples

preting lotto game) and horn-shaped good-luck charms – descendants of the phallic amulets of Pompeii.

Jewellery

The ancient art of engraving and cameo-making is still practised in Naples and in the factories of Torre del Greco on the outskirts. Spaccanapoli has several jewellers selling traditional designs, while the streets south of Corso Umberto and west of Via Duomo are the domain of gold- and silversmiths.

AMALFI COAST

The bright ceramics made around the Amalfi Coast, particularly Vietri sul Mare, are highly prized. Workshops *(botteghe)* are dotted along the coastal road, though it's not always easy to stop. Ravello and Amalfi have a good choice of shops selling quality ceramics. The **Amatruda family** (www.amatruda.it) operates the last of Amalfi's paper mills, producing handmade paper that is sold in beautifully packaged boxes all over town. Positano is known for its clothes, swimwear and sandals.

SORRENTO

The main shopping street, Corso Italia, is dominated by fashion, footwear and jewellery stores; the more up-market boutiques are west of Piazza Tasso. The narrow pedestrian streets of Via San Cesareo and Via Fuoro are full of souvenir shops, selling lemon-themed teatowels,

ceramics and soaps, as well as leather bags, lace and the ubiquitous *limoncello*. Marquetry *(intarsio)* is Sorrento's other speciality. For quality pieces, visit **A. Gargiulo & Jannuzzi** (Viale E. Caruso 1; www. gargiulo-jannuzzi.it).

CAPRI

The streets between the Piazzetta, Via Vittorio Emanuele and Via Camerelle are home to the top names in fashion. The prices are prohibitive for most, but window-shopping is a time-honoured Capri pastime. For a cheaper souvenir, visit **Carthusia** (Viale Matteotti 2d).

Naples' markets

Naples' street markets are great hunting grounds for foodie souvenirs – and offer an authentic slice of Neapolitan life in all its chaotic, colourful glory. Towards the station, the market around Porta Nolana is famous for its fish, but also sells fruit and vegetables. Via Pignasecca, the heart of working-class Naples, climbs from Piazza Carità (at the end of the pedestrianised section of Via Toledo) to Montesanto station. It's heaven for bargain-hunters and food-lovers, with its hotchpotch of fruit, fish and tripe stalls, bakeries and delis, and a great place to pick up salamis and cheeses. The tiny food shops and stalls along Via dei Tribunali are good for *taralli* (Neapolitan savoury pastries), biscuits, pasta and wine.

Teatro San Carlo

ENTERTAINMENT

Performance is part of Neapolitan life. The locals' innate flair for entertainment and penchant for theatrics are reflected in the city's cultural life, from world-class opera to classical concerts under the stars.

Naples is best known for its opera, but, as seems fitting for this earthy, down-to-earth city, it's the more populist, home-grown *canzone napoletana* that you're most likely to hear during your visit. Theatre in Naples is an Italian-only realm; the main venue is the **Teatro Bellini** (www.teatrobellini.it).

Plenty of concerts and events are organised, particularly in summer, but nightlife generally revolves around eating and drinking. The best way to enjoy the balmy nights is to join the locals for a postprandial stroll, with the essential ice-cream stop along the way.

MUSIC

Naples' Teatro San Carlo makes a grand backdrop to the world-class performances that take place there, while on the coast and islands, a concert with a view is not to be missed.

The **Teatro San Carlo** (www.teatrosancarlo.it) is the oldest working opera house in Europe and Italy's best after Milan's La Scala. The season runs from January to mid-July, and from September to December. Buy tickets in the theatre box office or from the ticket office in

Galleria Umberto I, opposite (www.boxofficenapoli.it).

Outside Naples, classical-music lovers are well catered for all summer long. During the Sorrento Festival, concerts are held in the picturesque cloister of San Francesco church, while the prestigious Ravello Festival (www.ravellofestival.com), centred on the Villa Rufolo gardens, draws an international crowd. In Capri, open-air concerts are staged at the Certosa di San Giacomo and Villa San Michele. The neoclassical villas in and around Ercolano play host to the Festival delle Ville Vesuviane (www.villevesuviane.net).

COMMEDIA DELL'ARTE

The *Commedia dell'arte*, in which stock characters play out a variety of plots on the eternal themes of love, jealousy, revenge and death, has ancient roots in Naples. Look out for Pulcinella – the female equivalent of Britain's Mr Punch – who crops up on any number of souvenirs, from puppets to key-rings, across the city. Performances these days are rare, but check www.guarattelle.it for details of forthcoming shows.

Evening concert at the Villa Rufolo gardens in Ravello

FILM

Virtually all English-language films are dubbed into Italian. Naples' film festival in June offers a rare opportunity to see films in their original language (www.napolifilmfestival.com).

NIGHTLIFE

The liveliest places after dark are the main piazzas of the old town, especially around the university district, where the majority of late-night bars and live-music venues are clustered. Chiaia, too, has a lively after-dark scene, with chic cocktail lounges and some trendy clubs; be sure to dress up. Listings of what's on where can be found in the local newspaper, *Il Mattino*, or drop in at the tourist office for information and free entertainment guides.

During the summer, many city venues close and beach bars turn into clubs. The best place along the coast for all-night dancing is Positano.

FESTIVALS

Each city, town and village has its own patron saint, and their feast day *(festa)* is celebrated with parades and processions, elaborate costumes, singing and dancing, fireworks and feasting. Summer is the season for classical-music festivals, most of which begin in July. Autumn festivals, known as *sagre*, are linked to the land and harvest time.

Annual events

The first major celebration of the year is Easter week, with large-scale Good Friday processions; Procida's is one of the most dramatic. In Naples, the thrice-yearly Festa di San Gennaro, the first of which is in May, is not to be missed if you're in the city. Also in May, the Maggio dei Monumenti allows access to historic buildings normally closed to the public (ask at the tourist office for a programme).

From July to September, open-air concerts take place in the spectacular Villa Rufolo in Ravello. July is a bumper month for saints' days: on the 16th, the bell tower of the church of the Madonna del Carmine on Naples' Piazza del Mercato explodes with fireworks; on the 26th, the patron saint of Ischia, Sant'Anna, is honoured with a torchlit procession of hundreds of boats; the 27th is the Festa di San Pantaleone, with the liquefaction of the saint's blood and a fireworks display in Ravello.

August 15 is Ferragosto (the feast of the Assumption) and a national holiday. Positano has a procession to commemorate the landing of the Saracens, followed by yet more pyrotechnics. September sees the Piedigrotta Festival, a traditional celebration of Neapolitan songs, as well as Pizzafest, a 10-day celebration of the doughy disc.

Finally, Christmas *(Natale)* in Naples is a colourful affair: churches compete to build the finest *presepe* (Nativity scene), and concerts are held around the city.

Popular beach at Báia

ACTIVITIES

This famed stretch of coast offers opportunities galore for outdoor types: hire a boat, take a diving course or stick to dry land and tackle one of the hiking trails that crisscross the countryside.

Naples' open spaces are perfect for running and cycling, but for swimming and watersports you're better off on the coast. Ischia is famous for spas. A full list of sports facilities in Naples, from bowling alleys to tennis courts, can be found on the tourist office's website, www.inaples.it.

SWIMMING

Most of the coastline from Naples to Salerno is rocky, as it is on the islands, and beaches are not always accessible or easy to find. In the Naples area, the cleanest water is at Posillipo, located west of town, although the beaches tend to be overrun in high season.

On the Sorrentine Peninsula, the Bay of Ieranto is many people's idea of a perfect, hidden-away beach; Sorrento itself is less blessed, though there are plenty of *stabilimenti* (beach clubs) where you can lounge around in the sun. Some of the fancier hotels in Sorrento and Amalfi have lifts down to the sea and their own seawater pools and private beaches.

The Amalfi Coast's grey-sand beaches are not the most picturesque, but Posi-

tano's and Amalfi's are broad at least, and the sea is clear enough.

Capri's shore, although pebbly, offers lots of opportunities for a dip; Marina Grande is the most accessible, but the section by the Blue Grotto is more appealing, with platforms carved out of the rock and ladders down to the sea.

Ischia has some lovely sandy beaches; the Baia di San Montano and the Spiaggia dei Maronti are the ones to head for.

On Procida, the Lido and Chiaia are the nicest beaches.

Super-fit swimmers compete in the Gulf Marathon (www.caprinapoli.com) every year in June, an epic 36km (22-mile) slog from Capri's Marina Grande to Naples' seafront.

DIVING

The Gulf of Naples offers plenty of opportunities for experienced divers and beginners alike, and there are a number of dive centres offering diving trips for around €70, courses and equipment. On the mainland, try Centro Sub Costiera Amalfitana (Via Marina di Praia, Praiano, tel: 089-812 148; www.centrosub.it).

If you can afford it, rent a boat

Walking to the beach

On Ischia, contact Ischia Diving Centre (Via Iasolino 106, Ischia Porto, tel: 081-981 852; www.ischiadiving.net). Procida's limpid blue waters are perfect for diving. Procida Diving Centre (tel: 081-896 8385 or 338-722 7484; www.vacanzeaprocida.it) organise dives with an instructor and equipment.

Diving in the Campi Flegrei is a particularly rewarding excursion (Centro Sub Campi Flegrei, tel: 081-853 1563; www.centrosubcampiflegrei.it), and the crystal-clear waters of the protected Marine Park of Punta della Campanella on the Sorrentine Peninsula is another popular spot. Futuro Mare (tel: 349 653 6323; www.sorrentodiving.it) organises daily excursions, including trips to the Marine Park and around Capri, Ischia and Procida.

BOATING

You can hire boats all along the coast. In Procida, try Blue Dream (tel: 081-896 0579; www.bluedreamcharter.com), which rents yachts and runs a sailing school. If a yacht is beyond your budget, try Ippocampo (tel: 081-896 77 64; www.ippocampo.biz), which rents dinghies and the local *gozzi* boats, as well as organising diving excursions, both day and night.

In Ischia, Capitan Morgan (tel: 081-985 080; www.capitanmorgan.it) runs inexpensive boat trips round the island and to other points on the coast. In Capri, Gruppo Motoscafisti (www.moto scafisticapri.com) operates boat trips round the island, while Capritime (tel: 329-214 9811; www.capritime.com) offers small-group boat tours with a skipper. For boat trips from Positano around the Amalfi Coast, read the 'Boat trips' box (see page 70).

WALKING

The Sorrentine peninsula, the Monti Lattari and Amalfi Coast, Ischia and Capri all offer scenic walking trails, many marked out by the Club Alpino Italiano (CAI). The maps of the Sorrentine Peninsula and Ischia and Procida published by Kompass are useful for hikers. Footpaths have also been marked out on the slopes of Mount Vesuvius and Monte Faito. Local tourist offices supply free walking maps.

For organised excursions, Giovanni Visetti (tel: 339-694 2911) is a friendly and knowledgeable local guide; his website, www.giovis.com, is an excellent resource.

RUNNING

The annual Naples Marathon (www.napolimarathon.com) is held mid-April, taking in the city centre and the Lungomare; there's also a half-marathon and a 4km (2.5-mile) fun run. If you just want a leisurely jog, the broad, sweeping Lungomare is perfect; alternatively, head for the unpolluted air of the Bosco di Capodimonte.

A victim of the AD 79 eruption at Pompeii

HISTORY: KEY DATES

Naples' history is woven into the city's fabric: the layout of the centro storico follows the grid of ancient Neapolis beneath it, while invaders from the French to the Spanish built churches and palazzi in distinctive architectural styles.

GREEKS AND ROMANS

*c.*700 BC	Greeks establish a colony at Parthenope.
474 BC	Greeks defeat the Etruscans and establish the new city of Neapolis near Parthenope. The two cities eventually merge to form one.
*c.*400 BC	Neapolis is commercial capital of Campania, northernmost province of Magna Graecia.
326 BC	Rome conquers Neapolis.
26 BC	Tiberius retires to Capri, from where he rules the Roman Empire.
AD 79	Vesuvius erupts, destroying Pompeii and Herculaneum.
324	Constantine becomes the first Christian Roman Emperor, ruling the Empire from Constantinople.

GOTHS, LOMBARDS AND NORMANS

536	Naples falls to the Eastern Empire.
568	The Lombards start to overrun Italy, and the south is divided between Byzantine and Lombard rulers.
1139	Naples falls to the Normans.
1194	Henry VI of Germany conquers the Norman kingdom of Sicily and becomes King of Naples.
1197–1250	Frederick, Henry's son, achieves absolute rule over the city, bringing good government and founding Naples' first university.

THE ANGEVINS AND ARAGONESE

1266	Kingdom of Naples given to the French royal house of Anjou.
1268	Charles makes Naples his royal residence.
1309–43	Robert of Anjou becomes King of Naples and brings Giotto and Petrarch to the court.

Louis XVIII meets Caroline   *Naples was bombed by the Allies during World War II*

1503	Naples is ruled by Spanish viceroys for the next two centuries.
1529	Plague rages in the city. Over 60,000 people perish.
1647	Poverty and oppression provoke a massive people's revolt led by a Neapolitan fisherman, Masaniello but violently quashed.
1656	Plague returns, claiming over 250,000 of Naples' inhabitants.

THE BOURBONS

1738	Austria loses power over the Kingdoms of Naples and Sicily to the Spanish Bourbons.
1806	Napoleon's brother, Joseph Bonaparte, takes control of Naples.
1815	Bourbons back on the throne after Napoleon's Waterloo defeat.
1860	Garibaldi defeats the Bourbons and enters Naples, making it part of a newly unified Kingdom of Italy.
1880–1914	More than 2.5 million Italians emigrate to the Americas.
1884	Severe cholera epidemic.

WORLD WAR II TO THE PRESENT DAY

1943	Naples is bombed by Allied forces. After a four-day uprising by the people, the German occupying troops are driven from the city.
1980	Campania is struck by earthquake, with 3,000 killed.
1994	Following the *Mani Pulite* (clean hands) anti-corruption campaign, Antonio Bassolino is elected mayor of Naples and begins a massive clean-up campaign.
2002	The lira is replaced by the euro.
2010	Prime Minister Silvio Berlusconi holds crisis talks in Naples to resolve ongoing mafia-related crime.
2011	Luigi de Magistris, a former mafia prosecutor, elected as Mayor of Naples.
2012	Allegations of blackmail, extortion and illicit contract manipulation regarding the city's waste management department arise.
2013	Berlusconi is convicted of paying for sex with an underage prostitute. Naples hosts the Universal Forum of Cultures.
2016	Luigi de Magistris is re-elected as mayor in June. Prime Minister Matteo Renzi loses a referendum on key constitutional changes in December, consequently resigns and is promptly replaced by Paolo Gentiloni.

BEST ROUTES

Via dei Tribunali

THE CENTRO STORICO

The atmospheric alleys of Naples' historic centre harbour many of the city's most intriguing sights, and give a real flavour of its exhilarating street life. Wander the ancient streets and feast your eyes: this is Naples at its heady, high-octane best.

DISTANCE: 3.5km (2.25 miles)
TIME: A full day
START: Piazza del Gesù Nuovo
END: Piazza Bellini
POINTS TO NOTE: You won't be able to visit all the churches mentioned in one day, especially as many close around noon, either for the rest of the day or until around 4pm. One option is to split the itinerary into two, allocating one morning to Spaccanapoli and another to Via dei Tribunali. If you're short of time, the must-sees are Santa Chiara, the Sansevero chapel, the Duomo and San Lorenzo Maggiore. The area is at its liveliest in the evening, so be sure to come back for dinner in one of the area's many pizzerias – a quintessential Naples experience.

Naples' *centro storico* is a dense network of shadowy, narrow alleys and small squares built on the site of ancient Neapolis. Fanning upwards from the harbour and bordered by Via Toledo to the west and Piazza Garibaldi to the east, the old town is crammed with everything from cavernous churches and grand *palazzi*, to cramped houses, shops and cafés. The most important sights are concentrated along two parallel east–west thoroughfares that formed part of the ancient street grid: Spaccanapoli and Via dei Tribunali.

SPACCANAPOLI

Spaccanapoli (literally, 'split Naples') is the series of narrow streets that run in a line from Via Toledo to the Greek walls.

Chiesa del Gesù Nuovo

The walk starts at Piazza del Gesù Nuovo, a bustling square dominated by the grey ashlar facade of the **Chiesa del Gesù Nuovo** ❶ (www.gesunuovo.it; daily 7.30am–1pm, 4–7.30pm), originally part of a Renaissance *palazzo* that was converted into a church by Jesuits in 1597. The Baroque interior is filled with frescoes, paintings and sculptures, including works by the Spanish artist José Ribera (1590–1652) and

Tiles at the convent of Santa Chiara

the master of Neapolitan Baroque Luca Giordano (1632–1705).

Santa Chiara

The first of Spaccanapoli's streets is Via Benedetto Croce. Immediately on the right stands the **convent of Santa Chiara** ❷ (www.monasterodi santachiara.com; church: Mon–Sat 7.30am–1pm, 4.30–8pm; cloister and museum: Mon–Sat 9.30am–5.30pm, Sun 10am–2.30pm). Although bomb damage during World War II destroyed much of the interior, reconstruction has preserved the austere character of the original church, built in the early 14th century for Robert of Anjou. His tomb lies behind the main altar. Fragments of a fresco by Giotto can be seen in the convent choir. The serene cloister, decorated with majolica tiles and planted with citrus trees, is one of the most photographed corners of Naples. A small museum displays a selection of liturgical objects salvaged from the bomb wreckage, but most interesting is the excavated area that reveals parts of an old Roman bath complex (1st century AD).

A few paces further on the right is **Gay Odin**, see ❶, a good excuse to stop for an ice cream.

San Domenico Maggiore

Next stop is Piazza San Domenico Maggiore, flanked by 16th- to 17th-century *palazzi* and the Gothic church of **San Domenico Maggiore** ❸ (church daily 9am–noon, 4.30–7pm). One of several churches commissioned by Charles I of Anjou, it was given a Baroque makeover in the 17th century, then remodelled in the 19th century in an attempt to restore something of its Gothic grandeur. The upper gallery of the treasury is lined with the tombs of kings and nobles of the Aragonese court. The inlaid marble altar and balustrade is by Cosimo Fanzago (1591–1678), leading sculptor and architect of his day.

Cappella Sansevero

Take a left turn up Via Domenico Maggiore, then right on to Via Francesco de Sanctis for one of Naples' unmissable sights, the **Cappella Sansevero** ❹ (www.museosansevero.it; Wed–Mon 9.30am–6.30pm). The burial chapel of the noble di Sangro family is crammed with sculptural monuments commissioned by Raimondo di Sangro, seventh prince of Sansevero (1710–71). The prince, a gifted scientist and inventor, was obsessed with alchemy – the two cadavers in the crypt are supposedly the product of one of his wild experiments. In the centre of the nave is the lifelike *Cristo Velato* (Veiled Christ) by Giuseppe Sammartino, sculpted in 1753. The rendering in alabaster of the soft folds and the translucence of the veil draped over Christ's prostrate body is remarkable.

Back on the square, stop for a coffee at the historic **Scaturchio**, see ❷.

San Domenico Maggiore

Via di San Gregorio Armeno

Proceed along Spaccanapoli (you are now on Via San Biagio dei Librai), past the recently restored **statue of the Nile ❺** on your left. The reclining figure is the Egyptian river god; the cherubs symbolise the river's tributaries. Peek into the tiny Bar Nilo opposite to pay your respects at the shrine to another revered figure, the Argentine footballer Diego Maradona.

If you're visiting at the weekend, find time to visit the lovely Cappella del Montedi Pietà, with a 17th-century frescoed ceiling and statues by Pietro Bernini on its facade. It's hidden away

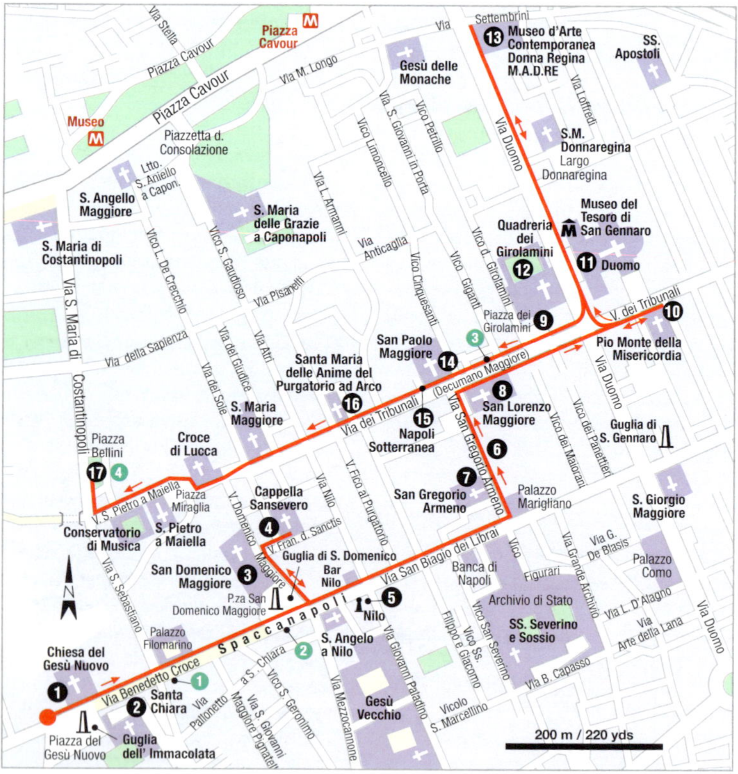

San Gregorio Armeno   *San Lorenzo Maggiore*

inside the Banca di Napoli at Via San Biagio dei Librai 114, and only open on Saturdays (9am–7pm), Sundays and holidays (9am–2pm).

A little further along, turn left into **Via San Gregorio Armeno ❻**. This narrow side street is entirely dedicated to the Neapolitan obsession with *presepi* – Christmas cribs. Stalls piled high with carved crib figurines, hand-crafted backdrops complete with ruins, trees and water features, fairy lights and baubles, lotto game boards and priapic good-luck charms spill out on to the street. Amongst the shepherds and wise men, look out for the modern-day heroes and villains, Barack Obama, Donald Trump, Silvio Berlusconi, Pope Francis and David Beckham among them.

If you reach the **church and convent of San Gregorio Armeno ❼** (Via di San Gregorio Armeno 1; Mon–Fri 9am–noon, Sat–Sun until 1pm, convent daily 9.30am–noon; free) before it closes, pop in to admire the interior, which is a riot of Baroque ornamentation, featuring frescoes by Luca Giordano.

San Lorenzo Maggiore

At the top of the street is the church of **San Lorenzo Maggiore ❽** (www.san lorenzomaggiore.na.it; daily 9.30am–5.30pm), another Angevin commission. Parts of the church, including the facade, were rebuilt in the 18th century, but most of the interior has been restored to its Gothic original. Skirting

the altar is a magnificent semicircular ribbed vault. Sections of glass in the transept floor reveal the remains of a Roman mosaic.

To see more of the Greco-Roman city that lies beneath, head down the steps to the **archaeological site** (daily 9.30am–5.30pm), where a section of the old Greco-Roman road has been excavated. It led to the forum or *agora*, still buried in the foundations of San Paolo church. Works have exposed the

Neapolitan *presepi*

No Neapolitan household would be complete without its *presepe* (crib) at Christmas, but in Naples, the Nativity scene is as crowded as the city streets, with an exuberant cast of extras – children, musicians, peasants, farmers, dogs and chickens – rubbing shoulders with the usual shepherds, kings and angels. Figurine carving is still considered an art form and even if you're not in Naples at Christmas time, you'll find plenty of opportunities to admire it. The artisans in Via Gregorio Armeno do a roaring trade, and many of the larger churches display *presepi* year-round, each with their own cast of Neapolitan characters, usually depicted with unforgiving realism, in contrast to the delicate execution of the saints and angels. Don't miss the wonderful examples in Santa Chiara and the San Martino monastery.

Via dei Tribunali flower shop

city treasure house *(aerarium)*, a dyer's *(fullonica)*, a laundry *(lavanderia)* and Roman market *(macellum)*.

VIA DEI TRIBUNALI

You are now on **Via dei Tribunali** (also known as the Decumano Maggiore), which arrows from Piazza Bellini to the Castel Capuano, and is as lively as Spaccanapoli, with the same dawn-to-dusk exuberance. Its abundance of excellent pizzerias makes Via dei Tribunali a good place to break for lunch; **Di Matteo**, see ❸, is one of the best.

Piazza dei Girolamini

Continuing east to **Piazza dei Girolamini** ❾, you'll come across some examples of the age-old local *rigattiere* (bric-a-brac) trade, with shops selling all manner of junk (or treasure, depending on your point of view), from Communion goblets to broken accordions and fragments of antique statuary – a good place to hunt for quirky souvenirs.

Pio Monte della Misericordia

Cross busy Via Duomo and continue on Via dei Tribunali for the small church and picture gallery of **Pio Monte della Misericordia** ❿ (www.piomontedellamisericordia.it; church and gallery: Mon–Sat 9am–6pm, Sun 9am–2.30pm), famous for Caravaggio's immense altarpiece, the *Seven Acts of Mercy* (1607). The upstairs picture gallery displays works by some of the leading lights of Neapolitan Baroque:

Luca Giordano, Massimo Stanzione and Giuseppe Ribera.

The Duomo

Back on Via Duomo, walk uphill to reach the **Duomo** ⓫ (Mon–Sat 8.30am–12.30pm, 4.30–7pm, Sun 8am–1.30pm, 5–7.30pm), whose ungainly neo-Gothic facade conceals a fine medieval building. The main attraction of the Baroque interior, in the **Cappella di San Gennaro**, is a precious silver bust containing phials of the blood of the city's patron saint. Three times a year (the Saturday before the first Sunday in May, 19 September, and 16 December), devotees flock to the Duomo to witness the liquefying of San Gennaro's dried blood. If the 'miracle' fails to occur, the superstitious say disaster will strike.

The chapel glitters with more silver busts of saints, an exquisite silver altar in relief and a gilded bronze gate by Cosimo Fanzago. Access to the baptistry (550 AD) and the Greek and Roman remains of previous buildings on the site (Mon–Sat 8am–12.30pm, 4.30–7pm, Sun 8am–1.30pm, 5–7.30pm) is from the left-hand nave. The next-door **Museo del Tesoro di San Gennaro** (www.museosangennaro.it; Mon–Sat 9am–5pm, Sun 9am–6.30pm) features paintings, silverware and ex-votos dedicated to the saint.

Opposite the Duomo, and reached through a lovely cloister planted with lemon trees, the small **Quadreria dei**

Duomo paintings

Scooting away

Girolamini ⑫ (Via Duomo 142; Mon–Tue and Thu–Fri 8.30am–7pm, Sat–Sun 8.30am–2pm; free first Sun of the month) has fine paintings from the 16th to the 18th centuries.

M.A.D.RE

Further up Via Duomo, turn right on to Via Settembrini for Naples' key collection of modern art: the Museo d'Arte Contemporanea Donna Regina, or **M.A.D.RE** ⑬ (www.madrenapoli.it; Mon, Wed–Sat 10.30am–7pm, Sun 10am–8pm; free on Mon). On the first floor are site-specific works by artists such as Anish Kapoor and Jeff Koons; look out also for Jannis Kounellis' gigantic anchor and Rebecca Horn's unsettling *Spiriti*, with swivelling mirrors concealing ranks of skulls, set to eerie music.

On the second floor is an impressive collection of works by contemporary greats on long-term loan – Andy Warhol, Jasper Johns and Damien Hirst among them. The complex also includes the finely restored 14th-century church of Santa Maria Donnaregina Vecchia, used for temporary exhibitions.

It's not signposted, but you can ask the staff at M.A.D.RE to show you to the roof terrace, where Mimmo Paladino's *Cavallo* ('Horse') sculpture lords it over the city below.

San Paolo Maggiore

Backtrack to Via dei Tribunali. About halfway along is the imposing church of **San Paolo Maggiore** ⑭ (church: Mon–Sat 9am–5.30pm, Sun 9.30am–1.30pm; free), built in the 16th century on the site of a temple to Castor and Pollux.

Napoli Sotterranea

Next door is the entrance to **Napoli Sotterranea** ⑮ (www.napolisotterranea.org; guided tours only, available daily in English 10am–noon, 2–4pm, at 6pm, Thu at 9pm by appointment only; duration of tour 90mins), a fascinating journey through underground Naples. Steps lead 40m (131ft) underground to the tunnels and chambers of the vast Greco-Roman aqueduct that supplied the city with its water until the cholera epidemic of 1884. Sections of the disused aqueduct were used as shelters during the heavy Allied bombardments of World War II. Claustrophobics beware – to reach one chamber you have to squeeze through some very narrow tunnels, lighting your way with a candle – but there's no better place to get a feel for the city's multi-layered history.

Santa Maria delle Anime del Purgatorio ad Arco

On the last stretch of Via dei Tribunali, the bronze skulls on the railings outside the 17th-century church of **Santa Maria delle Anime del Purgatorio ad Arco** ⑯ (church Mon–Sat 10am–5pm, museum and hypogeum Mon–Fri 10am–2pm, Sat 10am–5pm) indicate that this was no ordinary church. It was long used for the worship of the dead, a

practice officially forbidden by the Vatican, and the hypogeum still contains a pile of venerated bones.

Piazza Bellini

At Piazza Miraglia, Via dei Tribunali becomes Via San Pietro a Maiella, and passes the Gothic church of San Pietro a Maiella and the **Conservatorio di Musica**, with a lovely courtyard where the strains of students practising their instruments sounds like an orchestra tuning up; ask at the desk about performances in the recital hall. Turn right into leafy **Piazza Bellini** ⑰ and peer down at the section of Greco-Roman wall in the middle, before settling down to a well-deserved *aperitivo* on the shady terrace of **Intra Moenia**, see ④.

Food and Drink

① GAY ODIN

Via Benedetto Croce 61; tel: 081-551 0794; www.gay-odin.it; Mon–Sat 9.30am–8pm, Sun 10am–1.30pm; Closed Aug; €

This historic chocolatier and *gelateria* has been keeping sweet-toothed Neapolitans happy for over a century. Now with branches all over the city, it's a wonderful place to shop for edible souvenirs – the chocolates are delicious and the gourmet ice creams are just as tempting.

② SCATURCHIO

Piazza San Domenico Maggiore 19; tel: 081-551 7031; www.scaturchio.it; daily 7.30am–8.30pm; €

This long-established café not only serves an excellent cappuccino but is a great place to sample the classic Neapolitan sweets – *babà*, *sfogliatelle* and *pastiera*. The *ministeriali* – delectable coin-shaped chocolates stamped with the name of the bar's founder, Giovanni Scaturchio – look almost too good to eat.

③ DI MATTEO

Via dei Tribunali 94; tel: 081-455 262; €

Whether or not its claim to have invented the pizza margherita (on 4 April 1936, apparently) is to be believed, Di Matteo is the archetypal Neapolitan pizzeria: rowdy, chaotic and very, very cheap. Head upstairs to soak up the atmosphere and (appetite permitting) go for the house speciality, *ripieno fritto* (fried calzone).

④ CAFFÈ LETTERARIO INTRA MOENIA

Piazza Bellini 70; tel: 081-451 652; www.intramoenia.it; daily 10am–2am; €

With its prime position on pretty Piazza Bellini, this café-bookshop is a popular spot throughout the day for drinks, snacks and light meals such as omelettes, sandwiches and salads, but it comes into its own at *aperitivo* hour, when the tables on the plant-filled terrace are in high demand. Live music on Wednesdays at 9.30pm.

Castel Nuovo

ROYAL NAPLES

A full–day tour revealing Naples' monumental side. Marvel at the residences that were the hub of the Italian monarchy for over a thousand years, before joining the locals in a traditional seafront stroll.

DISTANCE: 5km (3 miles)
TIME: A full day
START: Castel Nuovo
END: Via Chiaia
POINTS TO NOTE: The R2 and C55 buses stop at Piazza Municipio. If possible, take this tour on a Sunday to join the Neapolitans out for their traditional weekly constitutional.

At the city's port, ferries and hydrofoils that shuttle commuters and day-trippers up and down the coast and across to the islands jostle for space with cruise and container ships. Standing guard over the port on traffic-choked Piazza Municipio is the Castel Nuovo (also known as the Maschio Angioino), the starting point of this tour.

CASTEL NUOVO

The Castel Nuovo ❶ (Mon–Sat 8.30am–7pm) was called the 'new castle' to distinguish it from its predecessors, the Castel Capuano and Cas-

tel dell'Ovo. Built for Charles I of Anjou in 1279, the Angevin castle became a centre of culture, attracting writers and artists, including Giotto, whose frescoes in the chapel and main hall are barely visible today. The Angevins were ousted by the Aragonese in 1443, and the castle was reconstructed under Alfonso I.

The interior

Sandwiched between two of the five cylindrical towers, the gleaming Renaissance **Triumphal Arch** is a testament to the cultural renewal of Naples by the House of Aragon. The doors depict the victory of Aragonese over Angevins; these are replicas of the original doors, which can be seen inside the museum, complete with embedded cannonball. The central relief panel above the entrance arch shows Alfonso's triumphant entry into the city.

Across the courtyard, the **Palatine Chapel** is all that remains of the original 13th-century structure, and is now part of the **Museo Civico**, which dis-

Paintings adorn the walls at the Palazzo Reale

plays mainly Neapolitan paintings, sculptures and bronzes from the 18th to the 20th centuries over three floors. Don't miss the stately **Hall of the Barons**, with its spectacular rib-vaulted ceiling that soars to a height of 28m (92ft). Named after a group of rebel-lious noblemen executed here by King Ferdinand I for plotting his murder, it is now more prosaically used for city council meetings.

According to legend, a crocodile was shipped in from Egypt to devour errant prisoners in the castle dungeon.

The grand interior of the Palazzo Reale

TEATRO SAN CARLO

Turn left out of Castel Nuovo and walk along Via Vittorio Emanuele to Via San Carlo and Piazza Trieste e Trento. Just before the square on your left is the **Teatro San Carlo** ❷ (www.teatro sancarlo.it; tours daily every hour 10.30am–12.30pm, 2.30–4.30pm, 45 mins duration), Italy's largest and oldest opera house, predating the Scala in Milan by 40 years. Commissioned by Charles of Bourbon in 1737 and completed in just eight months, it quickly became one of the most important social venues in 18th-century Naples – and the stage of many a scandalous liaison. The plush six-tiered auditorium, all red velvet and gold stucco, can seat up to 3,000. Tickets generally cost from €50 to €800, but watching a performance here is a rare treat. For more on the theatre's history, drop in on its new archive and museum, Memus.

VIA TOLEDO AND THE QUARTIERI SPAGNOLI

On the opposite side of Via San Carlo, underneath the arcade, is the main entrance to the **Galleria Umberto I** ❸. The magnificent glass-roofed gallery, built in 1890, is lined with smart shops and cafés; the western exit brings you out on to **Via Toledo** ❹, Naples' main shopping street.

The grid of streets leading west off Via Toledo make up the **Quartieri Spagnoli**

❺ (Spanish Quarter). Built to house the Spanish military, the cramped dwellings became home to Naples' working classes. The labyrinth of narrow streets, festooned with lines of washing, have become an evocative symbol of inner-city Naples.

PIAZZA PLEBISCITO

You will have spotted the traffic-free, semicircular Piazza Plebiscito by now. Before heading over there, stop for a coffee at **Caffè Gambrinus**, see ❶. In 1994, **Piazza Plebiscito** – the 'People's Square' – was reclaimed by the people. Until then, this magnificent square had been used as a car park, but was cleared of traffic as part of a citywide clean-up in the 1990s. The piazza is embraced by the twin arcades of **San Francesco di Paola** (daily 8.30am–7.30pm; free), an imposing neoclassical church inspired by the Pantheon in Rome. The two equestrian statues gracing the square commemorate the two Bourbon kings, Ferdinand I and Charles III; both are by Canova.

Palazzo Reale

Opposite the church, the **Palazzo Reale** ❻ (Piazza Plebiscito 1; www.palazzo realenapoli.it; Thu–Tue 9am–8pm, ticket office closes 7pm; free the first Sun of the month) is the highlight of this tour. Built in the middle of the 16th century, its design was tweaked on numerous occasions over the centuries, each ruler leaving his mark. The statues

Castel dell'Ovo

along the facade – the eight dynasties that ruled Naples from Roger the Norman to Victor Emmanuel of Savoy – present a potted history of the city.

Inside, a double staircase ascends to the **royal apartments**, resplendent with Baroque and neoclassical paintings, sculpture, tapestries and porcelain. The highlights are the **Court Theatre** (1768) and the **Royal Chapel**, which has a magnificent altar by Lazzari (1674), master of Neapolitan Baroque decoration, and a vast *presepe* (Christmas crib). The palace is also home to the **Biblioteca Nazionale** (www.bnnonline.it; Mon–Fri 8.30am–7pm, Sat 8.30am–1.30pm); its collection of books and manuscripts includes some 2,000 parchments from Herculaneum. The palace's hanging gardens (daily 9am–7pm, or 1hr before sunset in winter) are closed for restoration, but the garden to the left of the main entrance leads to another lovely one with views of the bay.

Before leaving the Palazzo Reale, it's worth checking out **Memus** (www.memus.squarespace.com; Tue and Thu–Sat 9am–5pm, Sun 9am–2pm), a new archive and museum showcasing objects used in performances at the city's opera house, the Teatro San Carlo.

SANTA LUCIA

Exit the square on Via Cesario Console, then turn right into **Via Santa Lucia ❼**, which cuts through the old fishermen's quarter and leads down to the sea. Rising above it to the right is the **Pizzofalcone** hill, site of the Greek settlement of Parthenope that predated Neapolis by three centuries.

Luxury hotels hog all the best views along Via Partenope, the road that skirts the bay. Nestled in the tiny harbour at the foot of the castle is the **Borgo Marinaro ❽**, an atmospheric enclave of seafood restaurants, romantically candlelit after dark, or a stunning spot for lunch, surrounded by bobbing fishing boats. Stop at **Antica Trattoria da Pietro**, see ❷, for a fish feast, or, alternatively, at **La Scialuppa**, (www.ristorantelascialuppa.it) next door.

Castel dell'Ovo

The **Castel dell'Ovo ❾** (www.castel-dell-ovo.com; Mon–Sat 9am–7.30pm, winter until 6.30pm, Sun all year 9am–2pm; free) is the oldest castle in Naples. It occupies a tiny islet named Megaris by the Greeks, who used it as a harbour.

The original fortress was built by the Aragonese in the 12th century, but most of the present structure dates from the early 16th century, when the citadel was rebuilt following its near destruction by the Spanish. Today, the castle is used to host cultural events and exhibitions, but the real appeal is exploring the battlements, gazing at the views.

According to legend, buried in the rock beneath the Castel dell'Ovo lies an ancient egg *(uovo)*, which holds the fate of the city within its shell. The Roman poet Virgil, believed to possess

The fortress–island   *Via Chiaia balcony*

powers of divination, prophesied that if the egg broke, catastrophe would befall the city.

THE LUNGOMARE

The broad stretch of road that sweeps around the bay from the castle, past the Villa Comunale to Mergellina, is punctuated at each end by a 17th-century fountain. A stroll along the seafront, or **Lungomare** ⑩, with an ice cream in hand, is a Neapolitan Sunday ritual.

The seafront has been designated a car-free area; to make the most of the space and the sea views, rent a bike or rickshaw from Foxrent Bike (Via Partenope 37/c; tel: 081-764 5060; daily 9am–8pm), almost opposite the Castel dell'Ovo.

CHIAIA

Continue along Via Partenope until you reach the park, then turn right into **Piazza Vittoria** ⑪ and follow boutique-lined Via Calabritto to **Piazza dei Martiri** ⑫, the epicentre of chichi Chiaia. Take the next left on to Via Alabardieri to reach **Enoteca Belledonne**, see ❸, before wandering back to Piazza Plebiscito along pedestrianised **Via Chiaia** ⑬, favoured by Naples' best-dressed for their evening *passeggiata*.

Food and Drink

❶ CAFFÈ GAMBRINUS

Via Chiaia 1–2; tel: 081-417 582; daily 7am–1am, later on Fri and Sat; http://grancaffegambrinus.com; €

This elegant Art Nouveau café, decked out with marble and chandeliers, dates from 1860. Once a popular haunt of artists, writers and politicians, it's now a time-honoured favourite for coffee and pastries during the day, early-evening *aperitivi* and pre-clubbing pick-me-ups.

❷ ANTICA TRATTORIA DA PIETRO

Via Luculliana 27; tel: 388 698 0996; daily 12.30–3pm, 7.30–10.30pm; €€

A refreshing and honestly-priced option for the Borgo Marinaro, with a handful of outdoor tables on the waterfront. The *gnocchetti di Pietro*, with calamari and olives, makes a delicious *primo*; follow with the daily fish special.

❸ ENOTECA BELLEDONNE

Via Belledonne a Chiaia 18; tel: 081-403 162; www.enotecabelledonne.com; Mon 4.30pm–1am, Tue–Sun 10am–1.30pm, 4.30pm–2am, Sun 7pm–1am; €

The early-evening crowds at this popular wine bar shun the tables in favour of the cobbled street outside. Come between 7pm and 10pm or after midnight for the best atmosphere – or outside of these times if you're after a quiet drink.

An exhibit at the National Ceramic Museum

CHIAIA AND VOMERO

A full day exploring the well-heeled and pleasantly airy districts of Chiaia, with its chichi boutiques, and Vomero, with its spacious avenues and knockout views, culminating in a stroll along the seafront to lively Mergellina.

DISTANCE: 6km (3.75 miles)
TIME: A full day
START: Piazza dei Martiri
END: Mergellina
POINTS TO NOTE: This is a good route for children. City Sightseeing buses run from Piazza Municipio to Castel Sant'Elmo, stopping at Chiaia and Piazza Vanvitelli in Vomero en route (Apr to Oct; several departures between 10am 5pm; €7; www.napoli.city-sightseeing.it).

Chiaia became fashionable in the 19th century and it remains a pocket of privilege from which its impeccably attired residents rarely stray. The Vomero hill above was just a sleepy village until the turn of the century. The building of elegant neo-Renaissance *palazzi* attracted wealthy Neapolitans, but after World War II, unregulated building covered most of the hill with modern blocks. Traces of its past endure, however, in a few handsome old buildings.

CHIAIA

Start at **Piazza dei Martiri** ❶, Chiaia's lively hub. Head north out of the square, veering left into **Via G. Filangieri**, which becomes Via dei Mille. Both streets are lined with exclusive shops and designer boutiques, with *palazzi* in between.

At Via dei Mille 60, the **Palazzo delle Arti di Napoli** ❷ (Wed–Sat and Mon 9.30am–7.30pm, Sun 9.30am–2.30pm; charge for exhibitions), or PAN for short, is a must for contemporary-art lovers. Exhibitions range from sculpture to photography to comics – and there's a great shop too.

The network of streets between this stretch and the Riviera di Chiaia yields more boutiques – Via della Cavallerizza and Via Poerio are particularly good. Via dei Mille runs into Via Vittoria Colonna, which ends at **Piazza Amedeo** ❸. The road to the right of the metro station here leads to the **funicular** ❹, which whisks you up to Vomero; get off at the last stop, **Cimarosa** ❺.

Riviera di Chiaia

Villa Floridiana

VILLA FLORIDIANA

Turn left out of the funicular station and walk along Via Cimarosa until you reach the **Villa Floridiana 6** (park 8am – 7pm).

Bench-lined paths wind past densely planted shrubbery, opening out on to a lawn – a favourite local picnic spot – and the Villa Floridiana. Once described as a 'Baroque chocolate box with neoclassical

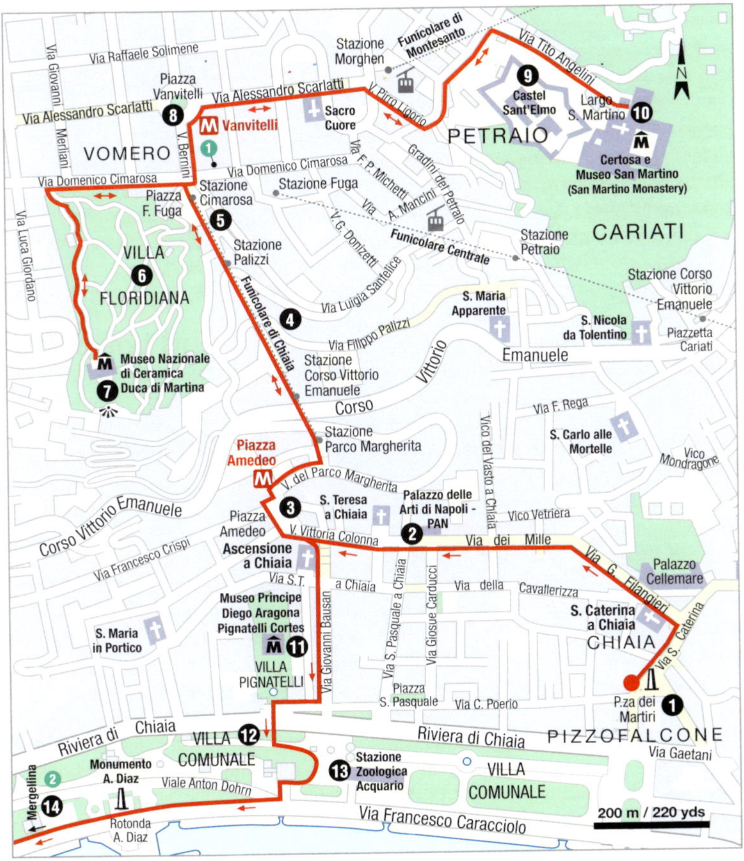

View from Castel Sant'Elmo

touches', it was a wedding present from King Ferdinand I to Lucia Migliaccio, his wife.

Museo Nazionale di Ceramica

The villa now houses the **Museo Nazionale di Ceramica Duca di Martina** ❼ (www.polomusealecampania. beniculturali.it/index.php/il-museo; Wed–Mon 8.30am–7pm, oriental porcelain 8.30am–4.45pm, European porcelain 9.30am–4.45pm, Renaissance and medieval art guided tours only, at 9.30am, 11.am, 12.30pm, 3pm, 4pm), with one of Italy's finest collections of fine china, including 18th-century porcelain from Meissen, Limoges, Sèvres and nearby Capodimonte, and an exceptional oriental collection. Before leaving Villa Floridiana, walk round the back through the gardens to the viewing platform at the bottom, which offers panoramic views of the city and the bay.

Back at the park gates, turn right onto Via Cimarosa and stop at **Acunzo**, see ❶, for lunch. Backtrack to the funicular and take Via Bernini, leading off it, to **Piazza Vanvitelli** ❽.

CASTEL SANT'ELMO

Take Via Alessandro Scarlatti, which leads off Piazza Vanvitelli to the right, climbing the two flights of steps up to the funicular station. Follow the road round to the right for the hulking **Castel Sant'Elmo** ❾ (entrance at Via Tito Angelini 20; www. coopculture.it; daily 8.30am–7.30pm,

winter 9am–5pm; free the first Sun of the month). Construction of the fortress was begun in 1329 by Robert of Anjou; in the mid-16th century, Spanish viceroy Don Pedro de Toledo added the six-pointed star shape, making the castle virtually impregnable. But in 1587 disaster struck when an explosion in the powder magazine all but destroyed it. The castle was gradually rebuilt and for many years served as a dungeon. Today the interior holds the **Museo del Novecento** (daily 8.30am–7.30pm), displaying local art from 1910 to 1980; more compelling is the staggering 360-degree view of the city from its battlements.

Back at the gate, turn right to continue the tour.

SAN MARTINO MONASTERY

Sharing the castle's hilltop perch is the **San Martino Monastery** ❿ (Largo San Martino 8; www.coopculture.it; Thu–Tue 8.30am–7.30pm; free the first Sun of the month), founded in 1325 but redesigned in the 17th century.

Cosimo Fanzago expanded the original **Angevin church**, giving it a Baroque makeover. He added a new facade and had the interior decorated with marble and paintings by the masters of Neapolitan Baroque.

A door at the back of the church leads to the **sacristy and chapter room**, with inlaid walnut panelling. You emerge from these sombre rooms into the bright **Chiostro Grande**, enclosed by a 64-column arcade

Opulent Villa Pignatelli

The port of Mergellina

of grey and white marble and a monks' graveyard, watched over by an eerie set of skulls ranged along a balustrade.

The **art gallery** is spread across two floors, its rooms facing on to the cloister on one side and offering more fantastic views of Naples on the other. Most of the 17th- and 18th-century works are housed in the former prior's quarters. Among the fine maps and landscapes, look out for the earliest pictorial record of Naples, the **Tavola Strozzi** (1465), showing the original monastery atop Vomero hill.

Backtrack to the Cimarosa funicular and return to Chiaia.

VILLA PIGNATELLI

From Piazza Amadeo, take Via Vittoria Colonna and turn right down the steps for **Museo Pignatelli** ⓫ (Via della Riviera di Chiaia 200; www.coopculture.it; Wed–Mon 8.30am–7pm, Tue 9am–2pm; free first Sun of the month). The neoclassical villa was built in 1826 for Ferdinand Acton, son of Ferdinand IV's prime minister. It was bought in 1841 by the Rothschilds, who sold it to the noble Pignatelli Cortes family.

VILLA COMUNALE

Crossing traffic-choked Riviera di Chiaia to the **Villa Comunale** ⓬, it's hard to imagine a time when this was a peaceful residential area. King Ferdinand IV cleared a block of buildings along here to turn his favourite strolling ground into a public park filled with exotic plants.

The **Stazione Zoologica Acquario** ⓭ (www.szn.it; Oct–Mar: Tue–Sun 9.30am–6.30pm; Oct–Mar Tue–Sun 9.30am–5pm) is Europe's oldest aquarium: built in 1874, it still contains the original 23 tanks.

MERGELLINA

Exit the park and follow Via Caracciolo west along the seafront to the port of **Mergellina** ⓮. On the opposite side of the marina is a line-up of kiosks – or 'chalets' – selling drinks and snacks; these include **Chalet Ciro**, see ❷.

Food and Drink

❶ ACUNZO

Via Cimarosa 60; tel: 081-578 5362; Mon–Sat 1–3pm, 7.30–midnight; €
The closely set tables at this unpretentious trattoria are taken up by locals enjoying pasta and pizzas; the house special is topped with sausage, *friarelli* (local greens), peppers, aubergine and cheese.

❷ CHALET CIRO

Via Caracciolo 31; tel: 081-669 928; www.chaletciro.com; Thu–Tue 6.30am–2.30am; €
Brace yourself for queue-barging at the legendary Chalet Ciro: for ice cream this good, the locals don't like to wait in line. The pastries are excellent too.

THE CATACOMBS AND MUSEUMS

This route explores the artistic and archaeological treasures of Naples' top two museums, and takes in some more offbeat sights en route, notably one of the area's subterranean cemeteries and the engagingly untouristic district of La Sanità.

DISTANCE: 2.5km (1.5 miles)
TIME: A full day
START: Museo di Capodimonte
END: Museo Archeologico Nazionale
POINTS TO NOTE: To get to the Museo di Capodimonte take bus R4 or C63 from the port or Piazza Dante, or bus 178 or 168 from Piazza Museo or line A of the City Sightseeing buses. There is also a shuttle bus between both museums (except Wed, www.napoli. city-sightseeing.it). You will need at least three hours for each museum, but the tour can be split up. The opening hours of the catacombs require you to set out early – a 9am start will allow you to see the Museo di Capodimonte first. Take an extra layer of clothing for the catacombs as they can be chilly, and watch your belongings in La Sanità.

When the noise and chaos of the city get too much for you, head for the Museo di Capodimonte and the Museo Archeologico. Between the two are a number of lesser-known sights, equally rewarding in their own way: the fascinating Catacombs of San Gaudioso and the workaday district of La Sanità.

MUSEO DI CAPODIMONTE

The **Museo di Capodimonte** ❶ (www. museocapodimonte.beniculturali.it; Thu–Tue 8.30am–7.30pm, Neapolitan Baroque exhibition daily only at 10am, noon, 3pm and 5pm, the 19th century section and the Borgia collection only by prior appointment; free first Sun of the month), one of Italy's finest art museums, sits in the hilltop haven of Capodimonte, in its own park. When he became king, Charles III of Bourbon gathered all the artworks he had inherited from his mother, Elisabetta Farnese, to Naples. The problem was where to house them. While on one of his hunting trips, the king decided that the hill to the north of the city, with its game-filled woods, was the perfect site for a hunting lodge and royal residence that would double as a museum for his precious collection. Building began in 1738, but progress was slow: the three-storey palace took 100 years to complete.

The imposing exterior of the Museo di Capodimonte

The core Farnese collection, rich in Renaissance art, was augmented by the Bourbon collection and subsequent acquisitions, many from churches and convents in the area. The collection now ranges Byzantine to contemporary.

Farnese Gallery

The visit begins with the **Farnese Gallery** on the first floor. The collection features some important early works – Masaccio's *Crucifixion*, a Botticelli Madonna and Filippino Lippi's *Annunciation and Saints* – but the 16th-century paintings are the cream of the crop. Highlights include *Antea* by Parmigianino, the portrait of an elegantly dressed young woman thought to be the artist's lover, and the monumental canvases by the Carraccis. The influence of Michelangelo is evident in the sculpted figures of Annibale Carracci's *Pietà* and in his Hercules at the Crossroads. Raphael is a dominant presence with his portraits of *Leo X and Two Cardinals* and *Cardinal Alessandro Farnese*. Pride of place is given to Titian's *Danaë*, which represents the mythical love scene from Ovid's *Metamorphoses* in which Zeus disguises himself as a shower of gold in order to seduce Danaë, daughter of the king of Argos. In the same room is *El Soflon* by El Greco, a mesmerising study of young boy blowing on a burning coal.

Galleria delle Cose Rare

The **Galleria delle Cose Rare** contains a sparkling display of rare and precious objects that once graced the Farnese palaces. The rooms beyond are taken up by Flemish paintings, mostly acquired by the Bourbons at the beginning of the 17th century, a mix of earthy, pastoral scenes and still lifes.

Royal apartments

Before heading up to the second floor, wander through the ornate **Royal Apartments** and marvel at the ballroom with its giant chandelier, and the Porcelain Parlour of Queen Maria Amalia, lined with over 3,000 tiles made in King Charles's porcelain factory.

Second floor

The second floor is given over to Neapolitan art from the 13th to the 18th centuries. Among the early works is Simone Martini's *San Ludovico di Tolosa*, a masterpiece of Italian Gothic art from San Lorenzo Maggiore. Central to the 17th-century works in the collection are the Caravaggio canvases, in particular the *Flagellation*, which was transferred from San Domenico Maggiore. This influential painting heralded a golden age of Neapolitan art, whose leading lights were Mattia Preti, Giuseppe de Ribera, Battistello Caracciolo and Luca Giordano, all represented. Don't miss the monumental d'Avalos tapestries, made in Brussels for the Habsburg emperor Charles V, to commemorate his victory over the French in the Battle of Pavia.

Caravaggio's 'Flagellation'

The gallery's modern-art collection starts on the second floor with Alberto Burri's *Grande Cretto Nero*.

Third floor

The third floor and part of the former attics are dedicated to modern and contemporary art. Don't miss Andy Warhol's iconic *Vesuvius*. Before leaving, browse in the prints and drawings gallery on the ground floor. Its 27,500-strong collection includes cartoons by Raphael and Michelangelo, and prints by, among others, Dürer and Rembrandt.

There's more contemporary art in the **Sala Causa**, off the courtyard, which holds big-name temporary exhibitions.

Parco di Capodimonte

Revive yourself with a coffee in the courtyard café and then take a stroll around the **Parco di Capodimonte**. The gardens were laid out in 1742 by architect Sanfelice, whose designs were influenced both by the formal French style and the Romantic English

style. Sanfelice was also commissioned to build the royal porcelain factory, which turned out top-quality porcelain until Charles dismantled the operation

Catacomb fresco   *Palazzo Sanfelice*

and transferred it, workers and all, to Spain when he returned there in 1759.

Take bus C63, 178 or 2M from almost opposite the entrance to the park and get off at the first stop after you pass the green-and-yellow tiled cupola on your left (or it's a 25-minute walk down the twisting road). Here you'll find a lift *(ascensore)* down to the district of La Sanità and, beneath the church of Santa Maria della Sanità, the Catacombs of San Gaudioso.

CATACOMBE DI SAN GAUDIOSO

The area beneath the park and down towards La Sanità is honeycombed with catacombs, which can be visited.

First tunnelled out of the rock by the Ancient Romans, who used them as water cisterns, the **Catacombe di San Gaudioso** ❷ (Piazza della Sanità 14; www.catacombedinapoli.it; daily 10am–1pm, hour-long guided tours only every hour, call to request a tour in English) were used as Christian burial sites from the 5th century onwards. Through the musty gloom you can still make out remnants of 5th- and 6th-century mosaics and faded frescoes: look out for the Christian symbols of the lamb, the peacock, and the bunch of grapes.

Your catacombs ticket also gets you entry to the two-level Catacombe di San Gennaro, at Via Tondo di Capodimonte 13 (guided tours only; hourly Mon–Sat 10am–5pm, Sun 10am–2pm), which are embellished with 2nd-century frescoes.

LA SANITÀ

Back above ground, explore **La Sanità**, one of Naples' most characterful districts: untouched by tourism, this appealingly rowdy network of streets is a great place to absorb yourself in the sights and sounds of the city. Follow **Via della Sanità** ❸ from the church. Full of the chaotic energy that characterises Naples and buzzing at all hours, this stretch offers as authentic a slice of Neapolitan life as you'll find anywhere in the city. The area is peppered with Catholic shrines – stop at Traversa Lammatari and look to your right for a typically overblown example.

Via delle Vergini

Just before the road veers left, peek into the courtyard of the **Palazzo Sanfelice** ❹ to your right to admire its magnificent – though sadly dilapidated – double staircases. Via della Sanità merges with **Via delle Vergini** ❺, site of a colourful local market (daily 8am–8pm), selling everything from flowers to frying pans. No. 19, **Palazzo dello Spagnuolo** ❻, holds another impressive double staircase, this one restored. A small museum dedicated to Totò, veteran comic actor and the area's most famous son is planned on the top floor.

Just off Via delle Vergini, on the Via Fuori Porta San Gennaro 13/14, you can stop for lunch at **La Campagnola**, see ❶, or, further down at Piazza Cavour, have a snack at

Museo Archeologico lion

Mignone, see ②, before moving on to the Museo Archeologico.

MUSEO ARCHEOLOGICO

At the far end of Piazza Cavour, the **Museo Archeologico Nazionale** ❼ (National Archeological Museum; Piazza Museo 19; www.museoarcheo logiconapoli.it or www.coopculture.it; Wed–Mon 9am–7.30pm, May–Sep Thu until 11pm; free the first Sun of the month) is an unparalleled collection of Greek and Roman artefacts. The museum occupies a hulking red *palazzo* on the northern outskirts of the *centro storico*. Originally the seat of Naples University, the 17th-century building was requisitioned in 1777 by Ferdinand IV to house the Farnese collection bequeathed to him by his father, Charles III of Bourbon. Charles's mother came from the aristocratic Farnese family whose members had assembled a vast collection of antique and contemporary art. Ferdinand wanted to gather as much of the scattered collection as he could under one roof with the aim of establishing a 'temple of wisdom and knowledge'.

Farnese collection

The Farnese collection of antiquities is spread across the ground floor. Many of the sculptures are in fact Roman copies of Greek masterpieces. The Farnese *Hercules* in the main gallery is a first-rate copy of a statue by the Greek mas-

ter Lysippus. At the opposite end stands the *Farnese Bull* (*c.*200BC), a monumental sculpture carved from a single block of marble. It depicts the death of Dirce, tied to a bull by Antiope's sons for the attempted murder of their mother. Both statues come from the Baths of Caracalla in Rome. Other highlights are the *Aphrodite Callipige*, admiring the reflection of her curvaceous rear; the bronze and alabaster *Artemis of Ephesus*; and the *Tyrannicides*, a copy of a 4th-century Greek original.

Leading off the main gallery is a room full of incised gems and intricate cameos, while in the basement is the museum's small Egyptian collection, part of which came from the Borgia family (closed for restoration at the time of writing).

Mosaics collection

The mezzanine floor is shared between a 200,000-strong coin collection on one side, and Roman mosaics and the 'secret room' of Pompeiian erotica on the other. The finest mosaics come from the houses of wealthy Pompeians, most notably the House of the Faun (named after the lovely bronze sculpture of a dancing faun, displayed on the first floor). The undisputed masterpiece here is the mosaic of the Battle of Issus, depicting Alexander the Great's victory over the Persian king Darius. Animals were a favourite theme and there are realistic portrayals of cats and dogs, exotic creatures from the Nile and marine life.

Museo Archeologico sculptures

Gabinetto Segreto

The so-called **Gabinetto Segreto** is the biggest draw; in high season, put your name on the list when you buy your entrance ticket to minimise waiting time. Until recently, the statuettes, reliefs, mosaics and frescoes displayed here were deemed too pornographic for public viewing; the entrance to the secret room is still manned to prevent under-12s from going in. The explicit images of sexual antics between men, women, nymphs, satyrs and, in one case, a god and a goat, will leave you in no doubt as to the Roman taste for eroticism. Phalluses abound in every shape and form; as well as symbolising virility and fertility, they were used as good-luck charms to ward off the evil eye.

First floor

All the rooms on the first floor lead off the central **Salone Meridiana**, a vast hall decorated with frescoes and paintings glorifying the Bourbon. Set into the floor of the Salone Meridiana is a meridian line decorated at calculated intervals with signs of the zodiac. At midday a shaft of light falls from a hole in the top right-hand corner of the room and hits the sign that corresponds to the time of year. Most of this floor is dedicated to the Vesuvian paintings, as well as items from Paestum and other sites of Magna Grecia. Highlights also include the 118-piece silver collection from the Casa del Menan-dro, part of a hoard found in a wooden chest together with gold jewellery, precious stones and silver and gold coins; the famous Blue Vase, a glass-cameo amphora from Pompeii; and a series of rooms containing bronze statues and a wealth of other finds from the **Villa dei Papiri** in Herculaneum.

If the day's sightseeing has given you a healthy appetite, head to **Osteria Da Carmela** (see page 99), a short stroll south along Via Santa Maria di Costantinopoli.

Food and Drink

1 LA CAMPAGNOLA

Via Fuori Porta San Gennaro 13/14 ; tel: 081- 457 663; daily 11am–3.30pm, 7.30–11pm; €

The décor here is simple, but this busy trattoria is hugely popular and well-priced. The excellent pizzas are the main draw here, especially the *calzones*, featuring four types of cheese. Also well worth a try is the sole, served with mozzarella, yellow cherry tomatoes, spicy salami and onions.

2 MIGNONE

Piazza Cavour 145; tel: 081-293 074; daily 24 hours; www.pasticceriamignone.it; €

This hole-in-the-wall *pasticceria* has all the Neapolitan classics – *babà*, *pastiera*, *sfogliatelle* – as well as gourmet chocolates. Perfect for a sugar hit before you tackle the Museo Archeologico.

Pozzuoli's Tempio di Serapide

THE CAMPI FLEGREI

This route covers the little-explored but fascinating Phlegraean Fields. Once mythologised by the ancients as the entrance to the Underworld, this area of geological quirks and archaeological wonders makes for a rewarding daytrip from Naples and is a good way to escape the crowds.

DISTANCE: 4km (2.5 miles) on foot and 20km (12.5 miles) by car/bus/train
TIME: A full day
START: Pozzuoli
END: Cuma
POINTS TO NOTE: The Campi Flegrei are well connected by public transport, and all major sights and attractions are served by buses and trains. By public transport, take a train from Naples' Montesanto station to Pozzuoli on the Cumana line or to Cuma on the Circumflegrea line (only three trains a day). From the Lucrino stop (Cumana line) take a bus to Baia. EAV buses run from Báia and Bacoli to Cuma. By car, take the Tangenziale (ring road) west from Naples through Fuorigrotta; exits are marked. A boat service runs from Molo Beverello to the Campi Flegrei in summer; see www.ilmattino.it for the timetable. Ferries run to Pozzuoli from Ischia and Procida (routes 11 and 12). The ground is uneven at Solfatara, so wear sturdy footwear.

The area west of Naples, between Pozzuoli and Cuma, is known as the **Campi Flegrei** (Phlegraean Fields), from the Greek *fleguròs* meaning fire. Back in the 8th century BC, when the first Greek colonists settled in Cuma, the volcanic terrain bubbled and hissed with the activity of some 20 now-extinct craters. Its ghostly atmosphere led the ancients to believe this was the gateway of the dead, and inspired Virgil and Dante to create their vision of hell. But such sinister associations didn't deter the Romans, who were drawn by the fertile land, mild climate and hot springs, and built villas and spas along the coast.

By the 1st century AD, the Campi Flegrei was one of the empire's most fashionable resorts – a far cry from its somewhat neglected modern-day incarnation: the Greco-Roman ruins lie buried under a sea of concrete. Picturesque it isn't, but ancient history still oozes from every street, port and hillside, and it is so far off the tourist trail that you may well find that you have the sights to yourself.

One of the Artecard tourist passes, 'Tutta la regione', gives you access to the

Yachts moored in Pozzuoli harbour

first two sights and half-price entrance to the rest for €32 (valid for three days, €34 for seven days), including transport. Alternatively, a €4 ticket will get you into the archaeological museum at Báia, Cuma and the Anfiteatro Flavio.

POZZUOLI

The starting point of this itinerary is the port of **Pozzuoli ❶**, which has three claims to fame: its Greco-Roman remains, its active crater and the fact that it is the birthplace of Sophia Loren. There's a lot of ground to cover, so get here as early as you can.

Tempio di Serapide

The Cumana train drops you near the port. Turn right from the station to reach the 1st-century market, or **Tempio di Serapide**, on the seafront, which was submerged in water until 1985 when the effects of bradyseism – the rising and falling of land levels caused by volcanic activity – left it uncovered.

Bubbling Solfatara

Rione Terra

Backtrack to the station and take Via G. De Fraia to your left to get to the centre, then turn left and walk up the hill for the **Rione Terra** (Sat–Sun 9am–7pm; ticket office closes 1hr earlier). Excavations resumed here in 2014 after a break, having previously uncovered a once-thriving ancient town, with remains of an Augustan temple, a bakery, a mill and slave lodgings.

Now head back downhill. For a snack in Pozzuoli, try **Caffè Serapide**, see ❶, in the central Piazza Repubblica. For something more upscale, join the throng on the esplanade, and walk to the end of the port to reach **Grottino a'Mmare** (see page 100).

Anfiteatro Flavio

Bus 152 runs from the opposite side of the piazza from the station to the **Anfiteatro Flavio** ❷ (Via Terracciano 75; www.coopculture.it; Wed–Mon 9am–1hr before sunset; ticket office closes 1hr earlier). This well-preserved amphitheatre held 40,000 spectators and was the third largest in the ancient world.

Solfatara

Bus 152 continues uphill to the **Solfatara** ❸ (Via Solfatara 161; daily 8.30am–1hr before sunset), a partially active crater in a strikingly lunar landscape. Volcanic activity is much more subdued since the crater was formed in 2000 BC, but you can still feel the heat, smell the pungent sulphur and get up close to the fumaroles, gas jets and bubbling mud.

Buses P9 and 152 run back down to the Cumana station, where you can take a train to Lucrino, then a bus to Báia.

BÁIA

Traces of an old Roman baths complex and adjacent temples are scattered along the **port of Báia** ❹, but you need to stretch your imagination to see this nondescript town as the luxurious spa it was. Much of the ancient resort lies under the sea due to bradyseism. At weekends in summer, glass-bottomed boats ferry tourists to the ruined villas under the water. Booking is obligatory on tel: 349-497 4183 or prenotazioni@baiasommersa.it.

In the area are some good restaurants; try **Da Papele**, see ❷.

Castello di Báia

The road out of the port winds round to Báia's main attraction, the **Castello di Báia**, now the **Museo Archeologico dei Campi Flegrei** ❺ (http://cir.campania. beniculturali.it/museoarcheologicocamp iflegrei or www.coopculture.it; Tue–Sun 9am–2.30pm, last entry at 1pm), sitting in splendid isolation at the tip of the headland, overlooking the Gulf of Pozzuoli. Built by the Aragonese, it was restructured by Don Pedro de Toledo after the 1538 eruption. Inside is an impressive collection of local archaeological treasures organised in chronological order, from sculptures found on the sea bed to

View from Castello di Bàia

Cuma's Cave of the Sibyl

fragments of Roman moulds modelled on famous Greek sculptures.

Buses run from Bàia to Bacoli; ask the driver where to get off for the **Piscina Mirabilis**. Call in advance, or ring the bell at the custodian's house on the corner of Via Piscina Mirabilis, for access (tel: +39 333 685 3278; daily 9am until sunset; free but tip expected). This immense cistern, carved out of the rock and supported by 48 pillars, held enough water to supply the Roman fleet anchored at Miseno.

CUMA

From Bacoli or Bàia get an EAV bus to the Cuma archaeological site ('Cuma Scavi'). From where the bus stops, walk up the hill past the **Archaeological Park**, containing remains of the ancient Roman bath complex.

The main archaeological site of **Cuma** ❻ (www.coopculture.it; 9am–1hr before sunset) is a little further up the hill. The first colony of Magna Grecia, it was founded in the 8th century BC by Greek traders based in Ischia. The finest sight is the Cave of the Sibyl, a long, echoing trapezoid corridor carved into the hill of the acropolis, pierced by shafts of light that fall through side openings. Legend has it that this was the domain of the sibyl, the prophetess in Virgil's *Aeneid* who guided Aeneas through the Underworld and predicted the fall of Rome. Steps lead up to the ruins of the **Temple of Apollo** and, higher still, the **Temple of Jupiter**, an ancient Greek sanctuary later

transformed into a Christian church. It's worth the climb for sweeping views over the surrounding woodland.

Buses run from the site to Fusaro Cumana station, from where you can take a train back to Naples. If you want refreshment before you leave, try **Giardini di Kyme**, see ❸.

Food and Drink

❶ CAFFÈ SERAPIDE

Piazza della Repubblica 94, Pozzuoli; tel: 081-012 3135; 7am–3am daily; €
A good menu of light meals and tables on a flower-filled terrace on the central square. Excellent pastries and ice cream.

❷ DA PAPELE

Via Lucullo 43, Bàia; tel: 081-1936 9921 ; Tue–Sun 1am–3pm, 6.30pm–midnight; €€
Pizza, salads and snacks are the order of the day at this informal pizzeria, pub and trattoria, located near the port. There's also a daily menu of *antipasti*, *primi*, and *secondi*. Good value for money.

❸ GIARDINI DI KYME

Via Montenuovo Licola Patria 131G, Cuma; tel: 331-580 3536; www.giardinidikyme.it; daily 7.30–11pm, Sat–Sun 12.30–3pm; €
Near the archaeological park at Cuma, this restaurant is set in beautiful gardens, with terraces offering fine views. The food is good too: try the baked razor clams or beef tagliata.

POMPEII, VESUVIUS AND HERCULANEUM

Explore Pompeii, one of the world's most evocative ancient sites, followed by a visit to Vesuvius, the volcano that obliterated the town. Neighbouring Herculaneum – smaller and quieter – is, for many, the most rewarding site of all.

DISTANCE: 35km (21.75 miles) on public transport plus 11km (7 miles) on foot
TIME: A full day
START: Pompeii
END: Herculaneum
POINTS TO NOTE: Between 2–3 hours at Pompeii should be sufficient to see the major sights; to explore in detail you need most of the day. You will need around 3 hours for Vesuvius. Circumvesuviana trains run along the Naples–Sorrento line to the Pompeii Scavi-Villa dei Misteri station, and also on the Naples–Poggiomarino line to the Pompei Santuario station. Vesuvius and Herculaneum can be reached from Ercolano Scavi station, which is on the Naples–Sorrento, Naples–Poggiomarino and Naples–Torre Annunziata lines. By car, take the A3 Naples–Salerno motorway, and exit at Pompei Ovest. To get from Pompeii to Vesuvius and Herculaneum, take the A3 towards Naples and exit at Ercolano. Sunscreen and sturdy shoes are essentials on this route. A picnic is the best lunch option.

When Mount Vesuvius erupted on the afternoon of August 24, AD 79, it had barely murmured for 800 years, so the destruction it caused is all the more startling.

At about 1pm, Vesuvius began to spew ash and stone thousands of metres into the air. The volcanic debris rained down on Pompeii, a thriving Roman town with a population of 20,000, smothering its buildings and inhabitants in a thick blanket of ash. Herculaneum, a humbler town to the west with fewer than 5,000 fishermen, craftsmen and farmers, and a few Roman aristocrats who had holiday homes there, was only mildly affected at this stage. Later that night, a scalding mixture of gas, ash and rock blasted Herculaneum; the town was then covered in a 20m (66ft) layer of mud.

Herculaneum was discovered by chance, in 1709, by a peasant digging a well; the first sections of Pompeii were unearthed by archaeologists of the Bourbon court of Charles III in 1748. The eruption effectively froze life in Pompeii as it was at the time, and the

Teatro Grande at Pompeii

site has probably yielded more information about the ordinary life of Roman citizens during the imperial era than any other. Its unique importance made it an essential stop for Europeans on the Grand Tour, and has captured the imagination of visitors ever since.

A combined ticket to Pompeii and Herculaneum costs €20, saving you €2 on the cost of separate tickets. The ticket also allows entry to the nearby archaeological sites of Boscoreale, Stabiae and the Villa Oplontis, and is valid for three consecutive days. In high season, the crowds at Pompeii can be overwhelming, and you can expect to queue to get into the major attractions. Get there as early as possible to avoid having to wait in line.

POMPEII

The entrance point to the ruins of **Pompeii** ❶ (www.pompeiisites.org and www.coopculture.it; Mon–Fri Apr–Oct 9am–7.30pm, last entry 6pm, Nov–Mar 9am–5pm, last entry 3.30pm, Sat–Sun from 8.30am;free the first Sun of the month) is ancient **Porta Marina** ❹. Make sure you pick up a plan of the excavations when you buy your ticket. As well as a detailed map of the site, it has timed itineraries that guide you round the most interesting sites, whether you have just a couple of hours or a whole day at your disposal.

The road leads through Porta Marina past the temples of Venus and Apollo and into the **Forum** ❸, the centre of public life. Straight ahead, the **Tempio di Giove** ❸ (Temple of Jupiter) is silhouetted against the dramatic backdrop of Vesuvius. To the left, inside the old granary stores, are displayed stacks of terracotta storage jars and plaster casts of carbonised victims.

North of the Forum

In the grid of streets north of the Forum, between the ruins of roadside tavernas and ordinary dwellings, a number of well-preserved Patrician villas reveal how the other half lived. The houses of the wealthy were walled around the outside for privacy. Light came from the open courtyards (atria) and porticoed gardens (peristyles), around which the richly decorated rooms were arranged. Two of the best examples of Roman domestic architecture are the **Casa del Fauno** ❹ (Via della For-

Villa dei Misteri fresco

tuna), named after the bronze statue of a dancing faun found here, and the nearby **Casa dei Vettii** (Vicolo dei Vettii), the home of rich wine merchants.

Villa dei Misteri

Make your way to the **Porta di Ercolano** in the northwestern corner. It's a pleasant walk along the Via dei Sepolcri, flanked with ancient funerary monuments, to the **Villa dei Misteri ❺**. This aristocratic villa outside the city walls is known for the brightly hued fresco cycle that decorates the triclinium walls, depicting the initiation ceremony of a young bride into the cult of Dionysus.

Via dell'Abbondanza

To explore the eastern end of town, head back to the Forum and the **Via dell'Abbondanza ❻**. This street, lined with shops and taverns and cut through with cart tracks, would have been one of the town's busiest thoroughfares.

East of the Forum

On the left, the **Terme Stabiane ❼** were the city's largest baths, with separate sections for men and women, each with its own changing rooms. The Vicolo del Lupanare leads from here to the **Lupanare ❽**, one of 24 brothels in the city. Opposite the baths, on the right, Via dei Teitri leads to two amphi-

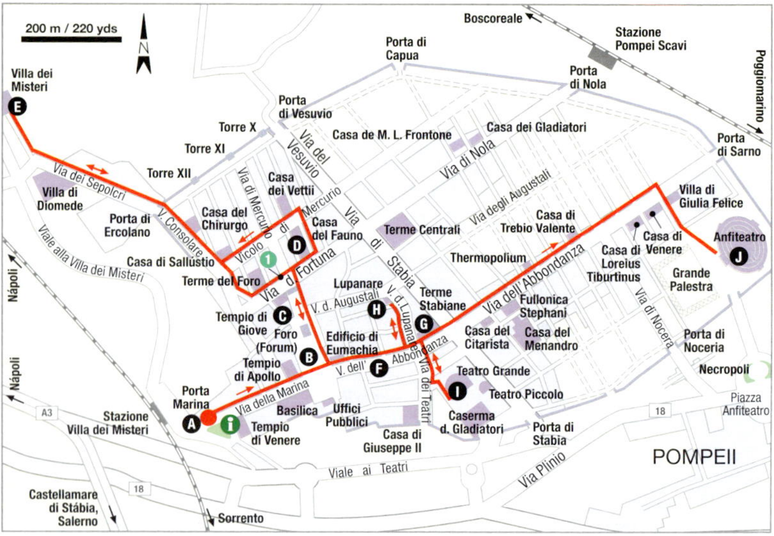

A volcano victim

Pompeiian statue

theatres: the **Teatro Grande** ❶ and **Teatro Piccolo**, where plays were performed and concerts and poetry readings given; the former is still the venue for performances and events from June to September.

Anfiteatro and Palestra

At the end of Via dell'Abbondanza is the main **Anfiteatro** ❿. This colossal arena could seat 15,000 spectators and was reserved for gladiatorial combat; the colonnaded **Palestra** next door was the gladiatorial training ground. If you've brought a picnic, this is the perfect place – you can sit on the terraces and imagine Nero giving the thumbs-down from his imperial box below. Alternatively, retrace your steps to the Forum and have lunch at the **Autogrill Café**, see ❶, behind the Temple of Jupiter.

VESUVIUS

Take the train to the Ercolano Scavi station, which is the stop for both Vesuvius and Herculaneum. A visit to **Vesuvius** ❷ (www.parconazionaledelvesuvio.it; Vesuvio; access to crater: 9am–2hrs before sunset; closed in bad weather), the only active volcano on the European mainland, makes a rewarding trip.

Climbing the crater

Vesuvio Express services (www.vesuvioexpress.it; daily 9am–4pm; tickets from the office to the left of the station; €10, without the entrance fee to the

path to the volcano) run from Ercolano Scavi station to Vesuvius every 30–40 minutes. The minibus winds its way up the fertile slopes to the summit, where the landscape becomes dark and barren, stopping 1km (0.5 mile) from the top at a car park, from where it's a 30-minute walk to the rim of the crater. The climb is not too extreme, but the winding lava-scree path is slippery, so take care. You can peer into the 200m- (650ft-) deep crater, but you can only go inside it on a guided walk.

Meet your minibus at the allotted time, and head back down to Ercolano Scavi station.

Pompeii in peril

Coachloads of tourists walk Pompeii's cobbled streets on a daily basis, ogling its chipped mosaics and snapping its faded frescoes. But Pompeii is now at risk for a second time: relentless foot traffic and the effects of the wind and rain on exposed ancient stones are taking their toll, and despite the site's importance, lack of investment has meant that priceless relics have been neglected for years. After a series of collapses, the Italian government declared a state of emergency, and in 2013 put in place a €150 million makeover – focused on reducing the risk of exposure to the elements and restoring the site's priceless frescoes – in a bid to preserve what remains.

Empty street in Herculaneum

HERCULANEUM

You may have reached saturation point by now, but a visit to **Herculaneum** ❸ (Ercolano; www.pompeiisites.org or www.coopculture.it; daily Apr–Oct 8.30am–7.30pm, last entry 6pm, Nov–Mar 8.30am–5pm, last entry 3.30pm; free the first Sun of the month) will prove highly rewarding. While most of Pompeii's buildings collapsed under the heavy downpour of rock and ash, in Herculaneum the upper floors of many of the houses withstood the force of the avalanche, and the dense coating of petrified mud encased and perfectly preserved their contents. It's a 10-minute walk downhill from the station, through the soulless modern town to the site; refuel at **La Fornacella**, see ❷, before you explore the ruins.

Cardo III and IV

Walk from the entrance along Cardo III to the **Casa del Tramezzo di Legno** Ⓐ (House of the Wooden Partition), so called because of the wooden screen separating the atrium from the *tablinum* (small office).

On the parallel Cardo IV, the **Casa a Graticcio** Ⓑ (the Trellis House) is a humble two-storey dwelling with a balcony.

North up the same street, the **Casa di Nettuno e Anfitrite** features a mosaic of Neptune; the next-door **Casa del Bel Cortile** Ⓒ (House of the Beautiful Courtyard) holds three of the 300 skeletons unearthed by archaeologists in 1980 – a mother, father and child huddling together for comfort. At the other end of Cardo IV, seek out the **Casa dell'Atrio a Mosaico** Ⓓ, an aristocratic residence with a geometric black-and-white mosaic on the atrium floor.

Cardo V

Cardo V holds the grandest house of all, the **Casa dei Cervi** Ⓗ (House of the Deer), named after the sculptures found in the garden. Beyond here is a scenic

Wall mosaics of Venus and Neptune

terrace that would have overlooked the sea. South of here, the **Terme Suburbane** ❺ (baths) are one of Herculaneum's best-preserved sites, complete with an intact Roman door – the only one on the site not charred by fire. On the site's eastern edge, the large **Palestra** (gymnasium complex) is where public games were held.

Villa dei Papiri

Recent excavations have concentrated on the **Villa dei Papiri** ❺, 150 metres west of the exit, named after the 200 carbonised papyrus scrolls found here. Though closed at the time of writing, its many artworks and artefacts, including the Dancers

of Herculaneum, can be seen in the Archaeological Museum.

Museo Archeologico Virtuale (MAV)

Near the entrance to Herculaneum at Via IV Novembre 44, the sleek **MAV** (www.museomav.it; June–Sept daily 10am–6.30pm, Oct–Feb Tue–Sun 10am–4pm, Mar–May daily 9am–5.30pm) takes you on a virtual-reality journey through various Roman ruins, such as the Forum at Pompeii, with computer-generated reconstructions and authentic sounds and smells to ensure an all-round sensory experience.

Vesuvius's eruptions

Following the catastrophic eruption, AD79, the plume of black smoke became a familiar sight on the skyline. Since its most recent eruption in 1944, however, when the cone collapsed into the crater, the volcano has been dormant, though fumaroles indicate a certain amount of activity. Today, its every movement is monitored by the Osservatorio Vesuviano (www.ov.ingv.it/ov), which has been recording data here since 1841 and celebrated the 175th anniversary of its foundation in 2016. You can climb to the rim safe in the knowledge that its expert vulcanologists are keeping a very close eye on things.

Food and Drink

❶ AUTOGRILL CAFÉ

Pompeii Scavi; tel: 081-536 4098; www.autogrill.com; daily, 8.30am–7.30pm; €

Pompeii's only restaurant may be an Autogrill (also found at many Italian service stations), but don't let that put you off: the Autogrill Café serves tasty quick lunches and snacks, together with good-value meal deals.

❷ LA FORNACELLA

Via IV Novembre 90–92, Ercolano; tel: 081-777 4861; www.lafornacella.it; daily 8am–11pm; €

This well-located bar-restaurant, 100 metres from the station on the road to Herculaneum, is ideal for a snack or a quick meal and does decent pizzas).

Sorrento harbour

THE SORRENTINE PENINSULA

A day and a night in the lively resort town of Sorrento, followed by a leisurely drive exploring the rugged Sorrentine Peninsula that divides the Bay of Naples from the Bay of Salerno.

DISTANCE: 23km (14.25 miles) on foot; 25km (15.5 miles) by car
TIME: Two days
START: Sorrento
END: Sant'Agata sui due Golfi
POINTS TO NOTE: Sorrento is easily reached from the Naples airport by Curreri coach (www.curreriviaggi. it), and by train from Naples on the Circumvesuviana line, but it's most fun to arrive by boat (from Naples' Beverello port). To explore the peninsula, you can either hire a car or a driver (www. benvenutolimos.com will tailor routes to suit you), or use the open-top City Sightseeing bus (www.sorrento. city-sightseeing.it), which covers the sights in this route. SITA buses run to Amalfi and Positano from Sorrento, and Marozzi buses to Rome.

The hook of land jutting from the southern end of the Bay of Naples is known as the Sorrentine Peninsula and forms part of the Monti Lattari range. Apart from Sorrento and a smattering of resort towns and hilltop villages, there is very little development, largely thanks to the inhospitable terrain in these parts. The craggy slopes are crisscrossed with ancient pathways and mule tracks that thread through olive and lemon groves into the hills and down to the sea.

SORRENTO

Travellers have been falling for the charms of **Sorrento** ❶ since ancient times: it was founded by the Greeks (the grid of streets in the old town is their legacy) and adopted by rich Romans who built luxurious villas here. It was rediscovered as a summer retreat in the 18th century, when the ongoing excavations of Pompeii made it an obligatory stop on the Grand Tour. Scores of distinguished visitors stopped off to pay a visit to the genteel resort, from Byron and Sir Walter Scott to Wagner, Henry James, Goethe and Ibsen. These days it's a lively resort town occupying a low-key middle ground between gritty Naples and the chichi resorts along the coast. Despite its lack of a decent

Duomo artwork   *Sedile Dominova*

beach, it's a good option for families, and has long been a favourite with British tourists.

Despite the crowds and tourist trappings, an air of elegance and romance prevails, and Sorrento's bustling, small-town street life makes it a rewarding place for an overnight stay.

The harbour

The most memorable way to arrive in Sorrento is by boat from Naples. Sorrento's harbour, Marina Piccola, huddles at the bottom of the long cliff on which the town is perched. Either walk south along Via Marina Piccola, then take the long flight of steps up to town, or hop on a bus from the harbour (buy your ticket from the information kiosk beforehand) up to Piazza Tasso. Most major hotels are within walking distance, but if you have luggage there are buses and taxis on the square.

Piazza Tasso

Sorrento's compact, walkable centre can easily be explored in half a day. Start at **Piazza Tasso Ⓐ**, the town's hub, flanked by bars and cafés, and busy day and night. Head west along busy, boutique-lined **Corso Italia**, stopping at **Primavera**, see ❶, the cream of the town's many *gelaterias*.

The Old Town

Continue west until you reach the **Duomo Ⓑ** (daily 8am–12.30pm, 4.30–9pm). Sorrento's cathedral is unremark-

able in itself, but the choir stalls show the local art of marquetry *(intarsia)* at its intricate best. Don't miss the lovely *presepe* to the left of the entrance, in which the news of Christ's birth interrupts the locals as they sit down to a fish dinner.

Beyond the Duomo, cross the road and venture into the old town. Running parallel to Corso Italia, the skinny **Via San Cesareo Ⓒ** is a riot of souvenir shops, hawking *limoncello* and a host of lemon-themed knick-knacks. On the corner of Via Giuliani is the **Sedile Dominova Ⓓ**, a beautiful 16th-century loggia, with a domed trompe l'œil cupola, that was the summer meeting place for Sorrentine aristocrats.

Villa Comunale

Walk downhill from here along Via Giuliani, turning right on to Via Vittorio Veneto, then left for the **Villa Comunale Ⓔ** (May–Oct 7am–midnight, Nov–Apr 7am–10pm), a shady park at the cliff's edge with wonderful views over the bay. At the edge of the park stands the Baroque church of **San Francesco Ⓕ** (daily 9am–1pm, 2–8pm) its bell tower topped with an onion dome. The medieval cloister makes a stunning venue for the classical and jazz concerts of the **Sorrento Festival**.

The beach

From the Villa Comunale, take the steps down to the beach platforms of **Marina Piccola Ⓖ**. Sorrento is

Villa Comunale offers great views

not known for its beaches, but if your hotel doesn't have a pool, the handful of public *stabilimenti* (Apr–early Oct), including Leonelli's Beach (www.leonellisbeach.com) and Marameo, (www.marameobeach.com), are well placed for soaking up the sun. You'll pay around €15 per day for entrance and a sun lounger, and most have a snack bar on site.

Basilica di Sant'Antonino

Back at San Francesco, take the road bearing left, which opens out on to Piazza Sant'Antonino, planted with shady palms and orange trees. Overlooking the square, the **Basilica di Sant'Antonino** (daily 7am–7.30pm) has an ornate Baroque interior, from

its chandeliers to its gold ceiling panels. Look out for the ex-votos from shipwrecked sailors: the local Saint Antoninus apparently rescued a child after it had been swallowed by a whale, and as such is the protector of those at sea. Outside the church, turn sharp right to reach the exceptional **Il Buco**, tucked into the church's stone vaults.

Museo Correale di Terranova

Back on the piazza, turn left to rejoin Piazza Tasso, left along Corso Italia and left again at the canary-yellow church into Via Correale. A five-minute stroll takes you to the **Museo Correale di Terranova** (Via Correale 48; www.museocorreale.it; Tue–Sat 9.30am–6.30pm, Sun 9.30am–1.30pm). The museum

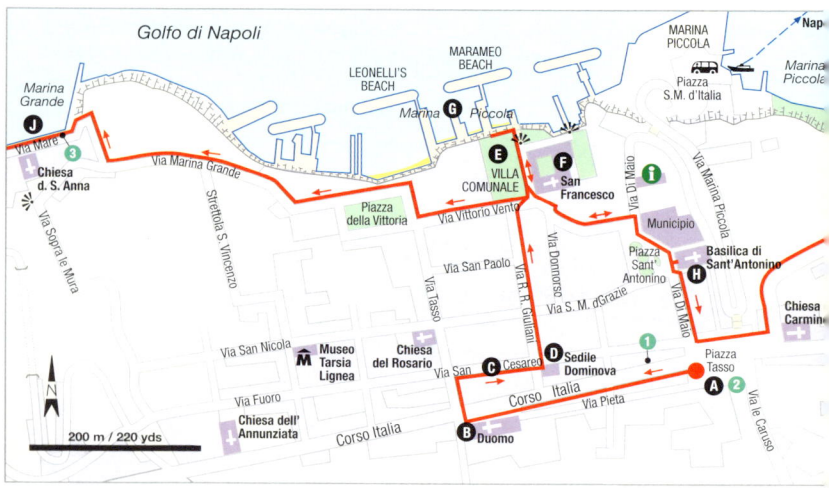

Beach life

Marina Grande

gets its name from brothers and art connoisseurs Alfredo and Pompeo Correale, counts of Terranova, who bequeathed their family's art collection to the city in 1924. Paintings by Neapolitan greats such as Luca Giordano and Giovanni Lanfranco, silverware, bronzes, *presepe* figurines, and a whole floor dedicated to porcelain and majolica make up the varied collection.

Marina Grande

Join the post-*passeggiata* throngs for an *aperitivo* in Piazza Tasso; buzzy **Fauno Bar**, see ❷, is the best place to kick off your evening. From here it's a 20-minute walk down to **Marina Grande** ❶. Make your way to Piazza della Vittoria and follow Via Marina Grande down to the harbour, confusingly called Marina Grande, the 'Big Port', as opposed to Marina Piccola, or 'Little Port': it is in fact the smaller and more down-at-heel of the two, but all the more charming for it. The tiny church of Sant'Anna in the harbour, with an array of ex-votos, is sometimes atmospherically candlelit at night.

The harbour is one of the most authentic corners of Sorrento. In the evening, the restaurants that hog the waterfront twinkle invitingly; for atmosphere, **Da Emilia**, see ❸, is hard to beat.

THE PENINSULA

Spend your second day exploring the Sorrento Peninsula. Exit Sorrento on Via Capo, which begins at the eastern end of Corso Italia. At the first fork turn right and follow the signs to Massa. The first stop is the small village of **Capo di Sorrento** ❷, where you can take the steep Roman road down towards the sea. It's a 10-minute walk past olive trees and oleander bushes to the ruins of the 1st-century **Villa di Pollio Felice**, spread across a precipice. A wooden walkway skirts the rocky coast to the Bagni della Regina Giovanna, a rocky beach with crystal-clear water.

Punta Campanella

The next settlement is **Massa Lubrense** ❸, actually 17 hamlets divided by olive

Sweeping view of the coast

groves. Make a pitstop in the square, admire the 16th-century Neapolitan paintings inside the church, and gaze at the view from the belvedere before moving on to **Termini** ❹, the departure point of one of the loveliest walks on the peninsula. Park outside the yellow church and follow the signs to the Punto Panoramico to reach **Punta Campanella** ❺. The road soon gives way to a footpath that descends slowly through terraced lemon and olive groves, past a Saracen watchtower, to the tip of the peninsula. The point is thought to be named after the warning bell *(campanella)* that was rung when Turkish pirates were sighted. The views from here are breathtaking and Capri is so close you could almost reach out and touch it. Allow for about two hours in total.

Bay of Ieranto

The coast from here to Positano is wild and rugged. The limestone cliffs sliced with deep ravines plunge into hidden coves that can only be reached by boat. It's largely inaccessible by car but a walker's paradise. The villages are linked by a series of footpaths that take you through citrus groves, chestnut and oak copses, and uninhabited areas blanketed in thick

Mediterranean vegetation; see www.giovis.com for routes.

Marina del Cantone is the only bay with a road link. On the winding road down to the bay is the sleepy village of **Nerano** ❻. From its piazza you can make the 45-minute walk along the cliffs to the **Marina di Ieranto** ❼, where you'll be rewarded with a spectacular beach.

Marina del Cantone

The road ends at **Marina del Cantone** ❽. It has a small, pebbly beach, but the real draw is its top-notch seafood restaurants, including the **Taverna del Capitano** (see page 101).

The peninsula is a walker's paradise

Sant'Agata sui due Golfi

The scenic road up to the town of **Sant'Agata sui due Golfi** ❾ is lined with olive groves, as well as myrtle, gorse and strawberry trees; even wild orchids thrive in this fertile soil. Sant'Agata is a nondescript town that has been put on the map thanks to one of Italy's most famous restaurants – gourmets travel for miles to sample the culinary masterpieces served up at **Don Alfonso 1890** (see page 101). The church on the same square has a beautiful altar inlaid with mother-of-pearl and lapis lazuli. Follow the signs 1km (0.5 mile) uphill to the **Il Deserto** convent (http://monachedeserto.alter vista.org; tel: 081-878 0199; call in advance to arrange access). The building looks more like a high-security

prison than a convent, but the views from the roof terrace are breathtaking. This is the only place along the coast from which you can see both the Gulf of Naples and the Gulf of Salerno, hence the name (*due golfi*: two gulfs). The road out of Sant'Agata joins the SS163; turn left to return to Sorrento or right to continue to Positano.

Monte Faito

In summer, visit Monte Faito for its lovely walks, cooling breezes and spectacular views. The *funivia* (cable car) is accessed from the Castellammare di Stabia stop on the Circumvesuviana line (Apr–Oct; every 20–30 mins). Bring a picnic, as there are no places to buy provisions beyond the funicular bars.

Food and Drink

POSITANO

The coast's most photogenic town offers welcome respite from a sights-packed itinerary. It's the perfect place to spend a few hours lazing on the beach, pottering around the shops and soaking up the atmosphere.

DISTANCE: 2km (1.25 miles)
TIME: Half a day
START: Upper town
END: Fornillo Beach
POINTS TO NOTE: There is no direct transport from Naples airport to Positano or any of the Amalfi Coast towns; private transfers cost upwards of €100. Alternatively, take a Curreri bus from the airport to Sorrento and pick up one of the blue SITA buses from Sorrento station to Positano (40 mins). In summer, ferries usually run to Positano from Sorrento and Naples, as well as from Ischia and Capri, so this route could be combined with routes 10 and 11, although the more traditional pairing would be with the Amalfi Coast drive (route 9).

With its near-vertical jumble of pastel-coloured houses clinging to cliffs that drop to a black-sand bay lined with rows of parasols, **Positano** is undeniably easy on the eye. Its charms have secured its place as the coast's most chichi resort, but stroll along the beach and you'll see that it's not entirely geared towards high-end tourism: among the serried ranks of pricey sun loungers, local families still spread out their towels and tuck into picnics.

The town became fashionable after World War II. 'Positano bites deep,' wrote a spellbound John Steinbeck. 'It is a dream that isn't quite real when you are there and becomes beckoningly real after you have gone.' Positano's quiet romance disappeared with the tourists that followed in Steinbeck's wake, though some of its old magic remains, especially after dark, when the town is lit up with fairy lights and restaurant tables spill out on to the stepped streets.

UPPER TOWN

SITA services drop off at the Sponda stop, from where it's a short stroll along **Via Cristoforo Colombo ①** to the lower town. If you're driving, leave your car in one of the car parks at the top end of town. Wend your way downhill.

Delightful Positano

LOWER TOWN

Steeply sloping **Via dei Mulini** ❷ heads down towards the sea; stop for a pastry at **La Zagara**, see ❶, before exploring the town. A little further down the street, peek into the beautiful flower-filled courtyard of **Palazzo Murat** on the left, once the residence of Joachim Murat, French king of Naples in the 18th century and husband to Napoleon's sister Caroline; it's now one of Positano's loveliest hotels (see page 93). Along this stretch and off the souk-like side streets are numerous boutiques, specialising in womenswear, leather sandals and swimwear.

Santa Maria Assunta

Via dei Mulini's overhead trellis hung with pink bougainvillea makes this a stunning approach to **Santa Maria Assunta** ❸ (Piazza Flavio Gioia; www.

chiesapositano.il; daily 8am–noon, 4–8pm). The church's Moorish green-and-yellow-tiled dome graces every postcard you'll see of Positano. Inside is the prized 13th-century Black Madonna icon, which is thought to hold the origins of the town's name – the story goes that when pirates tried to steal the figure, a booming command from Heaven to put it back 'posa, posa' ('put it down' in Latin) was supposedly heard.

Spiaggia Grande

Take the steps from the piazza down to the **Spiaggia Grande** ❹, the town's main beach and one of Positano's major draws – although the beach is shingly, the water is clean, and the beach is broad and backed by bars and restaurants. It can be very crowded in summer; expect to pay upwards of €20 for a day's sun lounger hire here. There is a small

spiaggia libera ('free beach'), a sun lounger-free patch that's popular with families, but this is inevitably towel-to-towel in high season.

Via Positanesi d'America

Take **Via Positanesi d'America** ❺, the seafront path that begins by the harbour and links the town's two beaches. The path winds along the bottom of the cliff, passing the Torre Trasita, one of the coast's many watchtowers, and **Lo Guarracino**, see ❷. The path also offers glorious views of the cluster of islets called **Li Galli**; thanks to its resemblance to a curvaceous woman floating in an azure sea, locals have nicknamed it Brigitte Bardot – appropriate for the place where Ulysses is thought to have been tempted by the seductive song of the sirens.

Spiaggia Fornillo

At the end of the path is **Spiaggia Fornillo** ❻, the beach named after the bakers' ovens used here in Roman times. It's more down-to-earth than the Spiaggia Grande, with a few low-key beach bars and restaurants. The Fornillo district clings to the hillside behind, its peaceful lanes a world away from the glitz of central Positano.

Boat trips

If there's one place on the Amalfi Coast that deserves to be seen from the sea, it's Positano. Several companies set up shop on the beaches in summer, offering day trips to Capri, along the Amalfi Coast, and to the **Grotta dello Smeraldo** (Emerald Grotto; Apr–Oct 9am–4pm, Nov–Mar 10am–3pm; last entry 30 mins before closing) – a shadowy grotto bathed in a shimmering emerald-green light – as well as sunset cruises to the Li Galli islands (although as this is private land, you can't go ashore). Alternatively, rent your own boat from around €60 per hour, or €70 per hour with skipper.

Food and Drink

❶ LA ZAGARA

Via dei Mulini 4; tel: 089-875 964; www.lazagara.com; daily 8am–1am; €

This local institution, named after the orange trees that grow on its interior terrace, has a tempting array of pastries; try the Zagara, a chocolate sponge cake made with tangerine syrup. Later on (at 9pm), La Zagara turns into a lively piano-bar.

❷ LO GUARRACINO

Via Positanesi d'America 12; tel: 089-875 794; www.loguarracinopositano.it; daily noon–3pm, 7–11pm; €€

This trattoria's scenic terrace, surrounded by olive and prickly pear trees, is what makes it special. Tasty pizzas and fish dishes are on the menu, as well as simple meat *secondi* such as veal escalope in lemon sauce. Booking is essential on summer evenings.

Amalfi rooftops

AMALFI AND RAVELLO

One of the world's most iconic drives, the serpentine Amalfi Coast road is breathtaking and nerve-jangling in equal measure. The tour takes in two of the coast's most picturesque towns, Amalfi and Ravello, and an optional hike in the beautiful Lattari mountains.

DISTANCE: 12km (7.5 miles) on foot, or 22km (13.5 miles) including the Sentiero degli Dei, plus 3.5km (2 miles) by car or public transport
TIME: Two days
START: Amalfi
END: Montepertuso
POINTS TO NOTE: The corniche coast road (SS163) requires nerves of steel – buses rocket round the bends with nonchalant ease, but only the most confident drivers should try the same. Traffic can be appalling in summer, so set out early. If you'd rather leave the driving to the locals, take the regular SITA bus service to Amalfi from Sorrento railway station (1hr 30 mins). Queue early for a window seat (on the right going out). There are frequent buses from Amalfi to Ravello (25 mins). In summer, boats run between Sorrento, Capri and the Amalfi Coast resorts.

The drive along the Costiera Amalfitana is one heart-stopping journey you won't forget. The 50km (31-mile) ribbon of road snakes its way between Sant'Agata sui due Golfi and Salerno, with vertiginous views of the sea below and the mountains above.

AMALFI

Having passed Positano (see route 8), the road winds its way round plunging valleys and soaring cliffs that drop almost sheer into the sea. The first major stop is cheerful **Amalfi ❶**. At the height of its power in the 11th century, the Maritime Republic of Amalfi rivalled the northern ports of Pisa, Genoa and Venice. Amalfitan merchants traded with Byzantium, Asia Minor and Africa, transforming their town into the most important port in southern Italy.

Nestling in a ravine, its tightly packed houses seem to tumble down to the tiny port below. Cars and buses park outside the city wall on Piazza Flavio Gioia.

Duomo and town centre

Pass through the arch into Piazza Duomo, dominated by the **Duomo Ⓐ** (daily July–Sept 9am–7.45pm, Mar–

Duomo statuary

June until 8.45pm, Oct–Feb 10am–1pm, 2.30–4.30pm), a striking example of Arab-Norman architecture. A steep flight of steps leads to the Moorish archways and facade inlaid with geometric mosaics – a 19th-century reconstruction of the medieval original. The bell tower (1276) and bronze doors, cast in Constantinople in the 11th century, are from the original structure, as is the **Chiostro del Paradiso** (1266). This atmospheric cloister with Arabesque arches was the cemetery of Amalfitan nobles. In the crypt lies part of the skull of St Andrew, patron saint of Amalfi.

Back on Piazza Duomo, stop for a sweet treat at historic **Pansa**, see ❶. The square is awash with day-trippers, but off the main drag you'll soon leave the crowds behind and lose yourself in the narrow, whitewashed side streets and covered alleyways. Among the countless souvenir shops is the odd gem, such as **Antichi Sapori d'Amalfi** (Supportico Ferrari 4; www.antichisaporidamalfi.it), a great place for souvenirs like fruity liqueurs in many flavours.

Walk back towards Piazza Flavio Gioia and to the **Antico Arsenale della Repubblica** ❷ (Largo Cesareo Console 3; Mar–Sept daily 10am–8pm, Oct–Feb Tue–Sun 10am–1.30pm, 3.30–7pm), a collection of old shipyards converted into an exciting new exhibition space, presenting works by modern masters such as Andy Warhol or Giorgio di Chirico. It's also the site of the **Museo della Bussola e del Ducato Marinaro di Amalfi**, which is dedicated

to Amalfi's heyday as a maritime republic and the history of the compass, which, according to local folklore, was invented by the Amalfitano Flavio Gioia in 1302. There are also other local memorabilia, as well as costumes from the town's historic regatta, the Festa delle Antiche Repubbliche Marinare, which is held annually in late May or June. Every four years, the Regatta of the Ancient Maritime Republics – Amalfi, Pisa, Venice and Genoa – comes to town, with a spectacular boat

Duomo interior   *Duomo façade and bell tower*

race ending in the harbour. The regatta was last held in Amalfi during 2016.

Paper Museum

Further north up the main **Via Pietro Capuano** , the tourist shops peter out, and once you reach Via delle Cartiere, Amalfi takes on an entirely different persona, more villagey and with the odd reminder of the industry that was once the town's big earner: 60 paper mills once operated here. The **Museo della Carta** (Paper Museum; Via delle Cartiere 23; www.museodellacarta.it; Mar–Oct daily 10am–6.30pm, Nov–Jan Tue–Sun until 4pm, closed Feb), gives demonstrations in the 13th-century paper mill downstairs.

Valle dei Mulini

Opposite the museum, the road that leads round to the right, then the steps up to the left lead to the **Valle dei Mulini** ('Valley of the Mills'), a wooded valley of wild flowers and waterfalls, which ends in terraced lemon groves: a walk of around an hour and a half.

ATRANI

From Amalfi's waterfront, it's a 15-minute stroll east to **Atrani**, a workaday place with some good, authentic trattorias. Walk past the Saracen tower (now the restaurant of the Hotel Luna Convento,

where Ibsen wrote *A Doll's House*) and around the headland to reach the beach. It has the same silvery sand as in Amalfi, but makes a much more peaceful place to laze in the sun. **Le Arcate**, see, right by the beach, is a lovely spot for lunch, after which you could explore Atrani's white-washed alleyways.

RAVELLO

Back on the coast road, take the left turn to Ravello, just past Atrani. The road climbs steeply for a few kilometres until the picture-perfect town comes into view, spilling down the hillside. Between the 11th and 13th centuries, wealthy merchants imported the Moorish artefacts and architectural styles that remain one of the town's glories.

Of the three main resorts along the coast, **Ravello** is the more refined and tranquil. Alternatively, buses usually run back down to Amalfi quite late, so you could have dinner here before heading back down; ask at the helpful

Al fresco dining in Ravello

tourist office for schedules (Via Roma 18bis; www.ravellotime.com).

The Duomo

The town is closed to traffic, so park outside and walk in. The bus from Amalfi stops outside a tunnel that leads straight to the main Piazza del Duomo, the archetypal small-town Italian square, with a handful of cafés and shops arranged around a medieval cathedral. The **Duomo** (www.chiesaravello.com; church daily 9am–noon, 5.30–7pm, museum daily 9am–7pm, winter until 6pm) is dedicated to St Pantaleone and holds two splendid Byzantine pulpits, one held aloft by six fierce lions, the other decorated with a mosaic of Jonah and the Whale. The attached museum holds sculptures, bronze artefacts and religious art.

Villa Rufolo and Villa Cimbrone

The real reason for coming to Ravello is its two lovely villas – or more accurately, their gardens. **Villa Rufolo ❹** (www.villa rufolo.it; summer daily 9am–8pm; winter daily 9am–sunset), in the shadow of the cathedral, was built in the Moorish style by the Rufolo dynasty, the richest family in medieval Ravello. Here, Wagner found inspiration for the magic garden in *Parsifal*, his last opera, in 1880. In summer, the luxuriant gardens host the prestigious Ravello Festival.

The town's other landmark is the **Villa Cimbrone** (www.villacimbrone.com; summer daily 9am–8pm; winter daily 9am–sunset), a pleasant 15-minute walk from

the square along narrow flower-filled streets. The villa was designed in the early 20th century by the eccentric Lord Grimthorpe, best known for designing the Westminster Clock. It is now a luxury hotel, but you can still visit the beautiful terraced gardens and the magnificent balcony, its balustrade lined with busts, hanging 300m (980ft) above sea level and offering stunning views.

Back in Piazza del Duomo, take Via Roma on the opposite side of the square for **Cumpà Cosimo** (see page 102), if you fancy a culinary treat.

PATH OF THE GODS

If you have a day to spare, consider venturing out on one of the many walking

Ravello festival

Every year, from July to September, sleepy Ravello adjusts to a huge increase in visitor numbers as it hosts the world-renowned Ravello Festival (www.ravello festival.com), a series of open-air concerts by prestigious performers. A concert under the stars in such atmospheric locations as Villas Rufolo and Cimbrone is a spine-tingling experience not to be missed by classical music fans. An added attraction is the space-age auditorium, designed by Brazilian architect Oscar Niemeyer. Ten years in the making, it offers both impressive acoustics and staggering views.

The Sentiero degli Dei

Cheerful ceramics in Ravello

trails that cut through the Monti Lattari. One of the best is the **Sentiero degli Dei** ❺ – the Path of the Gods, between the mountain villages of Bomerano, west of Amalfi, and Nocelle, east of Positano. .

Catch the earliest bus you can from Amalfi to Bomerano; the trail markings begin at the main square. It's a gentle three-hour walk through vineyards, lemon and cypress groves, and wild Mediterranean *macchia* (scrub) along a path suspended between sea and sky. The views are awe-inspiring. The walk ends at Nocelle, where the sky-high **Trattoria Santa Croce**, see ❸, serves wonderful home-cooking.

MONTEPERTUSO

If the walk has left you weak at the knees, take the bus from Nocelle to Positano via **Montepertuso** ❻. Alternatively, walk down to the centre of Positano (see route 8), from where there are buses to Amalfi.

On the descent to Montepertuso, look out for the huge hole that pierces a vast rock on the mountainside. As local legend has it, the hole was created by the Virgin Mary when the Devil challenged her to a contest: whoever pierced the rock would own the land. When Mary touched the rock, it crumbled, leaving a hole that swallowed her opponent up.

Food and Drink

❶ PANSA

Piazza Duomo 40, Amalfi; tel: 089-871 065; www.pasticceriapansa.it; Sun–Mon 7.30am–midnight; €

This historic *pasticceria* is an elegant spot for a coffee, lined with vintage wood cabinets and age-spotted mirrors. Be sure to try one of Pansa's citrus specialities: *delizia al limone*, stuffed with lemon cream and flavoured with *limoncello*, or chocolate-coated candied orange peel.

❷ LE ARCATE

Largo Cav. Orlando Buonocore, Atrani; tel: 089-871 367; www.learcate.net; Tue–Sun 12.30–3.15pm, 7.30–22.30pm, Mon only July–Aug; €€

Tucked into a corner of Atrani's harbour, Le Arcate's waterfront tables enjoy a location that can't be matched in Amalfi. The simple menu is strong on fish – grilled catch of the day with a simple salad makes a delicious lunch – and there are pizzas in the evening.

❸ TRATTORIA SANTA CROCE

Via Nocelle 19, Nocelle; tel: 089-811 260; www.ristorantesantacrocepositano.com; daily 12.15–3pm, 7–10pm, Sat–Sun only in winter; €€

Reward yourself after the Sentiero degli Dei with lunch at this tranquil restaurant. The antipasti plate makes a generous starter to share, and the mixed grill – the house speciality – is sure to replenish a few burned calories. Book a window table to make the most of the stunning views.

The Belvedere di Tragara

CAPRI

An overnight stay on one of the Mediterranean's most dazzling islands, taking in its two towns – glitzy Capri and lofty Anacapri – and walking its beautiful coastline, with panoramic views at every turn.

DISTANCE: 8.5km (5.25 miles) on foot plus 7.5km (4.5 miles) by public transport

TIME: Two days

START: The Piazzetta

END: Grotta Azzurra

POINTS TO NOTE: Hydrofoils and ferries to Capri depart regularly from Naples and Sorrento, and less regularly to Amalfi and Positano. Buy your return ticket early if you're not staying the night, as the later boats fill up quickly. Note that the Blue Grotto is closed if the sea is rough. Capri is hilly, so for the walks you'll need sturdy shoes. If you're planning to move around a lot, pick up a UnicoCapri day pass (€8.60), which covers unlimited bus journeys and a return journey on the funicular. Single tickets cost €1.80. Alternatively, get around on two wheels: Rent a Scooter, in Marina Grande (Via le Botteghe, 16 and other three sites; www.capriscooter.com; €30 for two hours or €50 per day) is by the harbour. The island's open-top taxis are plentiful but pricey.

With its soaring cliffs, emerald waters, lush vegetation and whitewashed towns, Capri is a capsule of Mediterranean beauty. The Emperor Augustus fell in love with the island when he arrived here in 29 BC and traded the fertile island of Ischia for this rocky paradise that had belonged to Naples. His adopted son Tiberius ruled the Roman Empire from here until his death. Capri's charms have been exalted by playwrights, poets and novelists through the ages, but these days, it is the island's jet-set glamour that is a magnet to visitors.

AROUND CAPRI TOWN

Boats arrive at **Marina Grande**. Before catching the funicular up to **Capri Town** ❶, buy tickets at the kiosk.

You emerge from the funicular on Piazza Umberto I. Known as the **Piazzetta**, this diminutive square, overlooked by the church of **Santo Stefano**, is the departure point for many lovely walks; the best is the 45-minute stroll up to Villa Jovis, the ancient ruins of Tiberius's palace on the eastern tip of

The Arco Naturale *Villa Jovis*

the island. Exit the square on Via Le Botteghe in the far right-hand corner and follow the well-marked route through the whitewashed streets, past walled gardens and olive groves. The climb is steep at points, but worth the effort for the views over the Bay of Naples.

Villa Jovis and the Arco Naturale

Villa Jovis ❷ (www.coopculture.it; opening hours vary, check website) was the grandest of 12 palaces that the emperor Tiberius had built on Capri. He ruled the Roman Empire from here for 10 years, between wild orgies and nights of debauchery. On the highest point is the **Salto di Tiberio** (Tiberius's Leap), from where the emperor hurled his enemies and unsatisfactory lovers. Nowadays it's an evocatively overgrown ruin.

On the way back down, when you reach the crossroads at the bottom of Via Tiberio, turn left into Via Matermánia and follow signs to the **Arco Naturale ❸**, a huge outcrop of limestone rock that has been eroded by the sea into a natural arch. Backtrack up the winding path to **Le Grottelle**, see ❶.

Belvedere di Tragara

From the restaurant, steps lead down to a coastal footpath and the **Grotta di Matermánia ❹**, a cave converted into a *nymphaeum* (fountain dedicated to water nymphs) by the Ancient Romans. Further along, the strange red villa balanced on the edge of a low-lying promontory to your left belonged to the writer Curzio Malaparte (1898–1957). The path ends at the terrace of the **Belvedere di Tragara ❺**,

Inside the Certosa di San Giacomo

with captivating views of the **Faraglioni**, a trio of rocks that are the habitat of the rare blue lizard.

Certosa di San Giacomo

It's a short walk back to the centre along Via Tragara and Via Camerelle, where you can browse in designer stores. At the top of Via Camerelle, turn left after the historic Hotel Quisisana into Via Serena, which leads to the **Certosa di San Giacomo** ❻ (Tue–Sun 10am–3pm). This medieval charterhouse is now home to a small museum, containing statues found in the Blue Grotto and paintings by the German Symbolist Karl Wilhelm Diefenbach.

Giardini di Augusto

Come out of the monastery and take the left-hand Via Matteotti at the junction with Via Serena for the **Giardini di Augusto** ❼ (www.coopculture.it; daily Apr–Oct 9am–7.30pm, winter 9.30am–5.30pm), which are terraced gardens offering more dazzling views.

At sunset, the Piazzetta regains its composure. Emptied of day-trippers, the little square turns into an outdoor salon as the *beau monde* emerges from the hotels for a night out. Join them for a cocktail; Piccolo Bar is the oldest and least showy of the quartet of bars. For dinner, the terrace at **Pulalli** (see page 104) can't be beaten.

AROUND ANACAPRI

Day two is spent exploring Anacapri and the west coast. Capri's second town is more rustic than its worldly rival, with a Moorish influence visible in its cubic whitewashed houses. Buses from Via Roma in Capri town run to **Piazza Vittoria**, which is crammed with souvenir shops.

In the piazza, walk up the steps and turn left for **Villa San Michele** ❽ (34 Viale Axel Munthe; www.villasanmichele. eu; Mar 9am–4.30pm; Apr and Oct 9am–5pm; May–Sept 9am–6pm; Nov–Feb 9am–3.30pm), built by the Swedish doctor Axel Munthe (1857–1949) on the ruins of one of Tiberius's villas. His book, *The Story of San Michele*, describing the building of his villa was an international bestseller. The house is now a museum with a display of ancient finds and eclectic furnishings, but the lush garden is the

---

Sentiero dei Fortini

To avoid the crowds, catch a bus from Anacapri to Punta Carena (take a bus signed 'Faro' from Via de Tommaso), one of the wildest corners of the island and the departure point for a stunning walk. The **Sentiero dei Fortini** hugs the west coast from the lighthouse at Punta Carena to the Punta dell'Arcera near the Blue Grotto, passing three ruined fortresses along the way. Mostly easy going, it takes about three hours each way. There are lots of places to swim en route, but returning ashore is not always easy, except at Punta Carena.

The view from Monte Solaro   *Lush garden at Villa San Michele*

highlight, with its vine-swathed pergola framing jaw-dropping views. It makes a spectacular venue for concerts under the stars in the summer. Don't miss the Egyptian Sphinx on the parapet of the chapel, on the garden's top level.

Monte Solaro
In the corner of Piazza Vittoria, a chair-lift whisks you up to the summit of **Monte Solaro** ❾ (589m/1,932ft; www.capri seggiovia.it; May–Oct 9.30–5pm; Mar–Apr 9.30am–4pm, Nov–Feb 10.30am–3.30pm). The wonderful, peaceful ride over gardens, woods and vineyards takes just under quarter of an hour, and more spellbinding views and a bar welcome you at the top.

Church of San Michele
Leading off Piazza Vittoria, Via Orlandi takes you to the Pompeiian-red **Casa Rossa** ❿ at No. 78 (Apr, May Tue–Sun 10am–5pm; June–Sept Tue–Sun 10am–1.30pm and 5.30–8pm; Oct Tue–Sun 10am–4pm), containing finds from the Blue Grotto. Continue on Via Orlandi, turning right on to Piazza San Nicola for the church of **San Michele** ⓫ (Apr–Sept daily 9am–7pm; Oct–Mar daily 10am–3pm), which is renowned for its majolica floor, depicting the expulsion from Paradise.

Grotta Azzurra
If you didn't succumb to one of the boat trips offered at Marina Grande, catch a bus to the **Grotta Azzurra** ⓬ Capri's big-

gest tourist attraction. Descend the steps to the cave entrance and join the queue for the boatmen who row endless streams of tourists around the marine cavern to admire the incredible glowing light within. The best time to visit is between 11am and 1pm, when the cave walls are bathed in an intense aquamarine light, while the sandy bottom glows with silvery shadows. The restaurant **Il Riccio**, see ❷, is just steps from the grotto.

Food and Drink

❶ LE GROTTELLE
Via Arco Naturale 13; tel: 081-837 5719; Apr–Oct 12–3pm, 7.30–11pm; €€€
Suspended above a verdant hillside overlooking the sea, this is an irresistible lunch spot. The food is delicious and unfussy, strong on fish dishes such as baked anchovies with local herbs. Booking is essential for the panoramic terrace.

❷ IL RICCIO
Via Gradola 4–6; tel: 081-837 1380; Thur–Sun 12.30–3.30pm, 7.30–10.30pm, Mon–Wed 12.30–3.30pm; www.capripalace.com; €€€
This chic waterside restaurant, in the swanky Capri Palace Hotel, has nautical decor and a classy menu. Awarded a Michelin star, it's big on freshly caught fish from an excellent seafood buffet. There's an on-site beach club, with secluded sun decks nestling among the rocks.

Lacco Ameno's Il Fungo

ISCHIA

This two-day tour of the lush 'emerald island' of Ischia does a loop of the island, taking in its bustling towns and stopping for a spot of pampering in its celebrated hot springs.

DISTANCE: 10km (6.25 miles) on foot plus 38km (23.5 miles) by car/bus
TIME: Two days
START: Ischia Porto
END: Ischia Ponte
POINTS TO NOTE: Hydrofoils and ferries depart from Naples, Sorrento and Pozzuoli to Ischia Porto, Casamicciola and Forio. The EAV bus from Ischia Porto covers the circular route described here about every 30 mins; the loop takes around two hours. The EAV follows the same route in the opposite direction; single tickets cost €2.50, and day passes are €6. Most hotels close from mid-October to Easter; published rates include half-board, but many will agree to bed and breakfast. Ischia is an easy place to navigate. The best way to explore is by car, although hiring a scooter can be fun too. Balestrieri Rent A Car (Via Iasolino 35; www.autonoleggiobalestrieri.it), behind the port to the right, charges from €30–50 per day for a car, €20–30 for a scooter.

Ischia may not have the same rugged beauty as its neighbour, but it has great beaches and protected inland areas that are a haven for walkers. As well as yielding excellent wine, the volcanic terrain produces bubbling hot springs, prized for their therapeutic powers.

Ischia was first settled by Greek traders in the 8th century BC, followed by the Romans who flocked to its spas. But less than a century after Pompeii, Monte Epomeo erupted, destroying all life on the island. From the Middle Ages, the islanders lived in fear of marauding Saracens, who remained a threat for centuries. It wasn't until the 19th century and the advent of the Grand Tourists that Ischia regained its status as a prestigious spa resort.

AROUND ISCHIA PORTO

Most boats from Naples stop at **Ischia Porto ❶**, a harbour whose natural boundaries once enclosed a volcanic crater lake. A string of fish restaurants lines the harbour.

This route follows the SS270 ring road in a westerly direction. **Casamicciola Terme ❷**, the first major town, has numerous spa hotels, but the best places are elsewhere.

LACCO AMENO

Carry on to **Lacco Ameno ❸**, site of the first Greek settlement. Just before the town beach, the SS270 veers inland, but continue along the seafront to admire the town's symbol, **Il Fungo**: a rock sculpted by erosion into a mushroom shape rising out of the sea. The road ends in a square with a pink church dedicated to the island's patron saint, **Santa Restituta**. The **Area Archeologica** next door (Mon–Sat 9.30am–12.30pm, June–Aug also 5–7pm, Apr–May and Sept–Oct 4–6pm) holds Greco-Roman remains.

Just off the square, a slope climbs to the 18th-century Villa Arbusto, home to the **Museo Archeologico di Pithecusae** (Corso Rizzoli 210; www.pithecusae.it; daily June–Sept 9.30am–1pm, 4–7.30pm; Oct–May 9.30am–1pm, 3–6.30pm) and more ancient treasures. The star exhibit is the 7th-century

Charming Forio

'Nestor's Cup', described in the *Iliad* and bearing one of the oldest Greek inscriptions in existence, praising the wines of Ischia.

NEGOMBO

The SS270 continues uphill, skirting **Monte Vico** (116m/381ft). This lofty promontory boasts the island's prettiest beach, the **Baia di San Montano**, and swankiest spa, **Negombo ❹** (Via San Montano 14; www.negombo.it), where 15 pools, caves and baths are arranged in terraces dotted with sculptures.

LA MORTELLA

Hidden among the signs at the next right-hand turning is one to **La Mortella ❺** (Via F. Calise 39; for tours tel: 081-990 118, www.lamortella.org; Easter–Oct Tue, Thu, Sat–Sun 9am–7pm), the estate of Eng-

lish composer Sir William Walton (1902–83). It is famous for its gardens, planted with 1,200 species and cultivated over 50 years by Walton's widow, Lady Susana, until her death in 2010. Concerts and Greek theatre performances are held here in spring, summer and autumn.

AROUND FORIO

Past La Mortella, the road carries on to the Spiaggia San Francesco, a little stretch of beach, then rejoins the SS270 at lively **Forio ❻**. Stroll into the historic centre along Corso Umberto and follow signs to the white church of **Madonna del Soccorso**, filled with offerings for the protection of fishermen and sailors. Nearby is the Michelin-starred **Umberto a Mare** (see page 105).

The nearest decent beach is **Citara**, most of which has been colonised by the **Giardini Poseidon ❼** (www.giardini poseidonterme.com). This spa has a more old-fashioned feel than Negombo, but its 21 pools and range of treatments make it popular.

For the chance to test some local wines stop by the **Pietratorcia Winery ❽**, see ❶.

SANT'ANGELO

Come off the SS270 at Panza and follow signs to **Sant'Angelo ❾** on the southernmost tip of the island; park outside the town. Sant'Angelo is not the untouched fishing village it once

Taking the waters

According to legend, an exhausted Ulysses regained his strength after wallowing in Casamicciola's hot springs, and Ischia's 103 springs and 67 fumaroles still do an excellent job of soothing weary limbs. Head for Negombo for cutting-edge treatments, Giardini Poseidon Terme and Aphrodite Apollon (www.aphroditeapollon.it) for mud baths and the spa at the Albergo della Regina Isabella (see page 95) for a more intimate spa experience.

Views over Ischia   *Castello Aragonese*

was, but something of its old character remains in the narrow streets and stack of pastel and white houses.

East of the village is the **Terme Aphrodite Apollon** spa (www.aphrodite apollon.it); beyond is the **Spiaggia dei Maronti**, a long stretch of public beach that can be reached via a clifftop footpath or by water taxi from the port.

MONTE EPOMEO

Back inland, the road winds its way up into the mountainous heartland. At the village of Fontana, take the first left after the little square, signposted for **Monte Epomeo** ⑩, which will take you halfway up the extinct volcano of Monte Epomeo, Ischia's highest point at 787m (2,582ft). Park at the bar and make the 40-minute trek to the top. Magnificent, 360-degree views of the island await you. Reward yourself with a drink at **La Grotta da Fiore**, see ②.

ISCHIA PONTE

The SS270 completes its circle at **Ischia Ponte** ⑪, where the hulking **Castello Aragonese** (www.castelloaragoneseis chia.com; daily 9am–sunset) lords it over the town. Park by the sea, then cross the Ponte Aragonese to the medieval castle.

The Greeks built the first fortress on this rocky islet in 474 BC. It was enlarged by subsequent rulers and, in 1441, Alfonso of Aragon strengthened the defences and added the bridge, enabling locals to take refuge within its walls during pirate

attacks. By the 18th century, the island had 13 churches and a thriving community, but in 1809, under French rule, it was bombarded by the British and all but destroyed. On July 26 each year, the Festa di Sant'Anna sees a spectacular seaborne procession staging the 'burning of the Castello Aragonese', culminating in an extravagant firework display.

Take the lift to the top, where you can wander a network of paths that take you past the ruined shells of churches, taking in the heart-stopping views from the ancient defences. If you want to wake up to that same view, book a room at **Il Monastero** (see page 96).

Food and Drink

① PIETRATORCIA WINERY

Via Provinciale Panza 267; tel: 081-907232; www.ristorantepietratorcia.it; Easter–Oct daily 11am–1pm, 4.30–8pm; €€€
Enjoy snacks or a full meal in a beautiful rustic setting at this renowned winery.

② LA GROTTA DA FIORE

Monte Epomeo; tel: 081-999 521; www.epomeolagrotta.com; Feb–Nov daily 9am–6pm, July–Aug by advance booking only; €€
The views are breathtaking from this trattoria on Monte Epomeo. They do rustic dishes such as *bucatini* pasta with Ischian rabbit and will ply you with *limoncello* until it's time to go back down.

PROCIDA

The low-key sights of the bay's smallest, least touristic island can be seen in a morning, followed by a lazy lunch in a picturesque marina, and an afternoon spent lounging on one of the unspoilt beaches.

DISTANCE: 6km (3.75 miles)
TIME: A leisurely day
START: Marina Grande
END: Lido
POINTS TO NOTE: Procida is a 40-min hydrofoil ride from Naples (leaving from Beverello) and 10 mins from Ischia. The ferry from Calata Porto di Massa takes an hour.

At just 4 sq km (2.5 sq miles), **Procida** is the smallest of the islands. Fishing and farming are still integral to its economy, and the volcanic soil is ideal for the cultivation of vineyards and citrus groves.

MARINA GRANDE

Ferries and hydrofoils dock at **Marina Grande** ❶, a colourful jumble of boats and sun-baked houses. The hill is dominated by the grim Castello d'Avalos, a prison until 1988. Turn left and meander along the harbour until you reach the church of **Santa Maria della Pietà** (1760) ❷. Stop for a coffee at the **Bar dal Cavaliere** opposite, see ❶, before taking Via Vittorio Emanuele uphill. Bear left at the yellow church to reach **Piazza dei Martiri** and the church of Santa Maria delle Grazie (1679).

It's a steep 500m climb from here to the crumbling **Abbazia San Michele Arcangelo** ❸ (Mon 10am–12.45pm; Tue–Sat 10am–12.45pm, 3pm–5pm; church free), which has a coffered ceiling decorated with gold and a painting of

Food and Drink

❶ BAR DAL CAVALIERE

Via Roma 42; tel: 081-810 1074; Tue–Sun 6.15am–1am; €
This *pasticceria* is a good place for a sweet treat – try the lemon or chocolate *lingua di bue*, a 'tongue' of flaky pastry.

❷ CRESCENZO

Via Marina Chiaiolella 33; tel: 081-896 7255; www.hotelcrescenzo.it; €€
This harbourfront restaurant serves the freshest of fish, right off the boat.

Marina Grande has a cheerful appeal

the Archangel Michael by Luca Giordano (1699). There's also a museum with an 18th-century *presepe* (crib) and a set of catacombs.

The whitewashed domes of the abbey church rise above the **Terra Murata**, the ruins of a once-impregnable citadel. On your way back down to the Piazza dei Martiri, stop at the terrace of the abandoned Castello and admire the view.

CORRICELLA

The fishing village of **Corricella ❹**, a warren of pretty pastel-painted houses interconnected by arches, can be reached via the sloping road by the church. Take the steps to the left of the pink house for the harbour, where fishermen mend nets and the day's catch is served up in bijoux fish restaurants.

Another set of steps at the far end of Corricella takes you back up to the main road. Turn left into **Via Scotti**, whose high-walled gardens offer tantalising glimpses of citrus trees. Continue along Corso Vittorio Emanuele, turning left off **Piazza Olmo** on to the quieter Via Pizzaco, which commands glorious views across the bay. A little way along on your left, a flight of steps leads down to **Chiaia ❺** beach, ideal for young children, and the family-run **La Conchiglia** restaurant (see page 105).

CHIAIOLELLA

Continue along Via Pizzaco, veering right into **Via de Gasperi**, and continue hugging the coast, enjoying views of Capo Miseno on the mainland, until you reach Via Solchiaro. Turn left then right into Via Simone Schiano, which leads to **Marina Chiaiolella ❻**, once the crater of a volcano and now a scene of yachts and fish restaurants; stop for lunch at **Crescenzo**, see ❷.

On the western side of the marina is the **Lido ❼**, Procida's longest and most popular beach. Buses L1 or L2 run from Chiaiolella back to the port.

DIRECTORY

Hand-picked hotels and restaurants to suit all budgets and tastes, organised by area, plus select nightlife listings, an alphabetical listing of practical information, a language guide and an overview of the best books and films to give you a flavour of the area.

The terrace at Grand Hotel Parker's

ACCOMMODATION

Naples' fanciest hotels are concentrated on the seafront (Lungomare) around Castel dell'Ovo and in Chiaia, but for atmosphere you might prefer one of the newer boutique hotels set in historic *palazzi* in the centro storico. Budget hotels cluster around the station, but this is not Naples' nicest corner; it's worth spending more to stay in the centre. Sorrento is a good base for exploring the islands and the Amalfi Coast, and Naples is only a 40-minute boat ride or one-hour train ride away from there. Accommodation in the bay area is generally pricey, especially on Capri and in the main towns of the Amalfi Coast, though in the last few years the area has seen some good-value B&Bs opening up, making a stay here viable for visitors on small budgets, too. Hotels get booked up well in advance, so reserve as early as possible; most hotels along the coast close between November and Easter, but may reopen for a few days over New Year.

Naples

Caravaggio
Piazza Sisto Riario Sforza 157; tel: 081-211

Price categories (for a double room in high season including breakfast):
€€€€ = over €270
€€€ = €170–270
€€ = €100–170
€ = under €100

0066; www.caravaggiohotel.it; €€
This small 4-star hotel with just 11 simple but comfortable guest rooms is set within a historic 17th-century building in a wonderfully convenient location behind the Duomo.

Decumani
Via San Giovanni Maggiore Pignatelli 15; tel: 081-551 8188; www.decumani.com; €€
This self-styled 'cultural hotel' is set in the one-time residence of Cardinal Riario Sforza: an elegant high-ceilinged *palazzo* with a breakfast salon that has to be seen to be believed. The rooms are spacious and tasteful, and the location in the heart of the *centro storico* is hard to beat.

Excelsior
Via Partenope 48; tel: 081-764 0111; www.eurostarsexcelsior.com; €€€
The grande dame of Naples' hotels, right on the waterfront, offers old-school glamour in spades. The rooms are spacious and wonderfully opulent, and the top-floor terrace is a lovely spot for breakfast or for a sunset cocktail in the summer months, offering sweeping views of the bay.

Grand Hotel Parker's
Corso Vittorio Emanuele 135; tel: 081-7612474; www.grandhotelparkers.it; €€€€
Founded in 1870, this grand hotel is away from the waterfront in fashionable

The Parker's lobby   *A suite at the Parker's*

Chiaia. The rooftop George's Restaurant and Bar offers candlelit dining at night, and heart-stopping views of Vesuvius and Capri by day. 82 rooms and suites.

Hotel Chiaja

Via Chiaia, 216 (1st floor); tel: 081-415 555; www.hotelchiaia.it; €€

Located close to Piazza Plebiscito, this endearingly old-fashioned, vintage-style hotel has ornately comfortable rooms quirkily decorated with antique furniture and is popular with musicians and artists performing at the nearby Teatro San Carlo. Staff are very helpful.

Exe Majestic

Largo Vasto a Chiaia 68; tel: 081-416500; www.exemajestic.com; €€

Set between the centro storico and Piazza Plebiscito, this is a very practical, convenient place to stay, offering comfort and convenience at a reasonable price but without much romance. It has a good buffet breakfast, plus a fitness centre. 112 bedrooms.

Micalò

Riviera di Chiaia 88; tel: 081-761 7131; www.micalo.it; €€€

Perfectly at home in chic Chiaia, this boutique hotel has a distinctly designer feel. Most of the rooms are on two levels, with stylish bathrooms up above. The acres of natural materials and modern neutrals are enhanced by an array of modern art by young Neapolitan artists on the walls. Excellent breakfasts, too.

Palazzo Decumani

Via del Grande Archivio 8; tel: 081-420 1379; www.palazzodecumani.com; €€

The sweeping spiral staircase at this boutique hotel sets the tone for the neo-Baroque decor throughout. The rooms are very comfortable, with luxuries such as plush chaises longues and marble bathrooms with Etro toiletries. The welcome cocktail is a nice touch, too.

Piazza Bellini

Via Santa Maria di Costantinopoli 101; tel: 081-451 732; www.hotelpiazzabellini.com; €€

Set in a historic palazzo, this hotel has been totally revamped and now boasts a fun, modern interior. The quirky sketches of a local cartoonist enliven the white walls, and the bright, contemporary rooms really make the hotel stand out among Naples' play-it-safe options. Staff are endlessly helpful and the location is a bonus – a stone's throw from leafy Piazza Bellini.

Santa Lucia

Via Partenope 46, 80121; tel: 081-764 0666; www.santalucia.it; €€€

One of a row of grand seafront hotels, in a prime position opposite the Castel dell'Ovo, which manages to be refined without being stuffy. Rooms are spacious, several have great views, and some have hot tubs.

Tribù

Via dei Tribunali 339; tel: 081-454 793; www.tribunapoli.com; €

Fantastic views over the harbour at Vesuvi

In the heart of the *centro storico*, this small, stylish B&B is run by arty couple Gaetano and Alessandra, who are full of suggestions on how to plan your stay. Rooms are thoughtfully furnished, with interesting art and design touches, and breakfast is taken on the sunny terrace in fine weather. No credit cards.

Grand Hotel Vesuvio

Via Partenope 45; tel: 081-764 0044; www.vesuvio.it; €€€€

With a prime position on this five-star strip, the Gran Hotel Vesuvio stands out for its charmingly old-fashioned feel and direct views of the Castel dell'Ovo. The rooms are as luxurious as you'd expect, and breakfast is a sumptuous banquet overlooking the waters of the bay. The Neapolitan tenor Caruso was a frequent guest.

Camping in Naples

A list of campsites in Naples and surrounding areas can be found at www.camping.it/en/campania/napoli. Most sites get very crowded in summer, so book in advance.

Naples Complesso Turistico Averno

Via Montenuovo Licola Patria 85, Pozzuoli; tel: 081-804 2666; www.averno.it; €

Attractive site with restaurant, bar, tennis, pool and hot-water thermal. Open all year round.

Sorrento

La Badia

Via Nastro Verde 8; tel: 081-878 1154; www.hotellabadia.it; €€

A small, pleasant (albeit basic) hotel in a lovely restored abbey surrounded by citrus groves, on the clifftops above Sorrento town. Pool, restaurant and fabulous views. It's a steep walk but there are regular buses. 41 rooms.

Casa Astarita

Corso Italia 67; tel: 081-877 4906; www.casastarita.com; €–€€

Right on Sorrento's lively main drag, this family-run B&B has individually furnished rooms, each decorated with a different colour scheme. You can use the library in the shared sitting room, and the free juices and water are a nice touch. Breakfast – with homemade cakes and jams – is a highlight.

Crowne Plaza Stabiae

SS 145 Sorrentina, km12, Castellammare di Stabia; tel: 081-394 6700; www.crowneplazasorrento.com; €€

An old cement works imaginatively converted into a stylish resort hotel with modern interiors, a fine pool and spa near Vico Equense on the Sorrento coast. Getting here is a little problematic, but the food alone is worth it – being some of the best in the bay area. The prices for a standard double are at the lower end of this price category.

Grand Hotel Excelsior Vittoria

Piazza Tasso 34; tel: 081-877 7111; www.exvitt.it; €€€€

The Vesuvi Presidential Suite

The most refined of the grand clifftop hotels, the magnificent Grand Hotel Excelsior is separated from the riff-raff on busy Piazza Tasso by its beautiful, flower-filled gardens. There are elegant salons, terraces with stunning views of the bay, a breakfast room with a wonderful frescoed ceiling and a lovely pool surrounded by greenery. The hotel was once home to the great Caruso (with his suite available for special bookings). It's worth paying extra for a room with a sea view.

La Tonnarella
Via del Capo 31; tel: 081-878 1153; www.latonnarella.it; €€
This clifftop villa is good value, and one of only a few on the coast open all year. A quiet hideaway, yet only a 10-minute walk into town. A few rooms have pine-shaded terracotta balconies and panoramic bay views. Small private pebble beach (with bar) is reached by a lift. Excellent restaurant and lunch can be served on the beach.

Ulisse Deluxe Hostel
Via del Mare 22; tel: 081-877 4753; www.ulissedeluxe.com; €€
Thanks to the 'hostel' tag, Ulisse is off many tourists' radar, but banish all thoughts of dingy dormitories: a hostel in name only, this place has spacious private rooms with all mod cons, a swimming pool in the basement and a perfect location, midway between the town centre and the beach. 50 rooms, including doubles, triples and quadruples. Male and female dormitories.

Amalfi

Floridiana
Via Brancia 1; tel: 089-873 6373; www.hotelfloridiana.it; €€
In a tranquil courtyard off Amalfi's heaving main street, this hotel has won awards for its customer service. The rooms are slightly old-fashioned in style, though none the worse for it; No. 3 is the biggest of the standard rooms, but it's worth paying the extra €10 for a bigger 'superior', or €20 for a two-level 'junior suite' with hydromassage bath.

Grand Hotel Convento di Amalfi
Via Annunziatella 46; tel: 089-873 6711; www.ghconventodiamalfi.com; €€€€
A former monastery on the Amalfi cliffs, with delightful gardens and an Arab-Norman cloister to add to its panoramic views. The renovation has been carried out with style, creating a deluxe contemporary haven with marble bathrooms, with some features intact from the original monastery.

Hotel Luna Convento
Via Pantaleone Comite 33; tel: 089-871 002; www.lunahotel.it; €€€€
Ibsen penned much of The Doll's House in this converted 13th-century monastery. In summer, breakfast is served in the Byzantine cloister, and rooms and the pool area (the pool is adjacent to the sea

Excelsior Vittoria bay view

and is filled with sea water) enjoy wonderful views.

Marina Riviera

Via P. Comite 19; tel: 089-871 104;
www.marinariviera.it; €€€€

This family-run four-star hotel, set on a cliff overlooking the sea, has built up a loyal clientele thanks to its excellent service and attention to detail. Some of the rooms have been given a glamorous revamp, while others boast a more old-fashioned, breezy seaside décor. The beach is just a couple of minutes' walk away, but with the pool, the terrace on the sea and solarium, you might just be tempted to stay put. The hotel's gourmet restaurant, Eolo, is highly regarded.

Sant'Alfonso

Via Sant'Alfonso 6, Furore; tel: 089-830 515; www.agriturismosantalfonso.it; €

A stay in this excellent *agriturismo*, well off the tourist trail but only 8km (5 miles) from Amalfi, is a wonderfully peaceful experience. Set high up in the mountains with stunning views, this is a serene retreat with eight comfortable, cosily decorated rooms, welcoming hosts and heart-stopping views. There's a good on-site restaurant too; the food is accompanied by wine from the farm's vineyards. Resident goats and geese complete the bucolic scene.

Santa Caterina

Strada Amalfitana 9; tel: 089-871012;
www.hotelsantacaterina.it; €€€€

Owned by the same family for generations, this is another of the coast's venerable hotels, carved into multiple levels of a cliff. Old-world and comfortably elegant, the hotel has a saltwater pool, lush terraced gardens, glorious views, a small private beach and respected restaurant – all further enhanced by a warm, helpful staff. An easy walk from town. 66 rooms and suites.

Positano

Buca di Bacco

Via Rampa Teglia 4; tel: 089-875 699;
www.bucadibacco.it; €€€€

With an excellent beachside location, acres of majolica tiles and antique furnishings, the Buca di Bacco has long been one of Positano's most desirable hotels. The rooms are traditionally furnished, though pale shades and French windows leading to sea-view balconies (in most rooms) give them a breezy feel. The hotel doesn't have claim to a section of beach, though a solarium is available for sun-worshippers.

Casa Albertina

Via della Tavolozza 3; tel: 089-875143;
www.casalbertina.it; €€

This pretty family-owned guesthouse is not for the weak of knee: there are 300 steps down to the beach, but it has exceptional views. Some rooms with balconies and Jacuzzis. Compulsory half-board in high season. 20 rooms.

Hotel Rivage

Via Capo 11; tel: 081-878 1873;

Excelsior Vittoria suite

The pool at Santa Caterina

www.hotelrivage.com; €€
A great budget hotel on the western edge of town. Most rooms have small terraces facing the water, and there's a pleasant restaurant with panoramic views.

Palazzo Murat
Via dei Mulini 23; tel: 089-875 177;
www.palazzomurat.it; €€€
With an impressive historic pedigree – this was the home of Napoleon's brother-in-law Joachim Murat, who was also King of Naples – this beautiful hotel has been run by the same family for generations. Heirlooms and cool tiled floors set the tone; request a room in the older, more charming main part of the hotel. The lovely central courtyard, nestled among palm trees, trailing bougainvillea and other Mediterranean blooms, makes a lovely spot for breakfast, and for candlelit dinners.

Palazzo Talamo
Via Pasitea 117; tel: 089-875 562;
www.palazzotalamo.it; €€€
Fresh, bright rooms are painted in restful pastel hues that take their cue from the traditional majolica floor tiles. All have sea views and private terraces; those on floor minus-2 are the best. Family-run, the service is excellent, and there are several very good restaurants along this stretch, too.

Pensione Maria Luisa
Via Fornillo 42; tel: 089-875 023;
www.pensionemarialuisa.com; €–€€
Run by the ever-enthusiastic Carlo, this budget hotel has a friendly, welcoming feel. It's tucked away in a warren of whitewashed alleys in the Fornillo district – so walking back from the beach involves a slog up steep flights of steps. All of the rooms are pleasant and spotless, but it's definitely worth paying the extra €10 for one of the rooms with a huge sea-view terrace. Unusually, it's open all year. No credit cards.

Poseidon
Via Pasitea 148; tel: 089-811111;
www.hotelposeidonpositano.it; €€€€
The Aonzo family proudly runs this hillside hotel, one of Positano's most pleasant and popular. Removed from the day-tripping buzz yet accessible to everything, it has a pool, beauty centre, gym and good restaurant. All rooms have terraces and lovely views. 48 rooms. Open early April to early January.

Le Sirenuse
Via C. Colombo 30; tel: 089-875066;
www.sirenuse.it; €€€€
This beautiful luxury hotel is set in an aristocratic 18th-century building in town above the beach. There are museum-quality family heirlooms throughout, wonderful open views of the sea and town, a stylish spa, an outdoor pool and a refined restaurant. 58 rooms.

Villa Franca
Via Pasitea 318; tel: 089-875655;
www.villafrancahotel.it; €€€
First-rate family-run hotel with well-decorated and comfortable rooms, most with tiled floors and arched windows that look onto the sea. Pool with magnificent views.

Ravello

Palazzo Avino
Via San Giovanni del Toro 28; tel: 089-818181; www.palazzosasso.com; €€€€
Formerly known as the Palazzo Sasso, this 12th-century aristocratic home has a gorgeous clifftop setting. One of the most fashionable and chic hotels around. Rooms are expensive, but they all have breathtaking sea views and are worth the premium. The food at the one-Michelin-star restaurant Rossellinis is magnificent. 43 rooms. Open March to October.

Parsifal
Via Gioacchino D'Anna 5; tel: 089-857 144; www.hotelparsifal.com; €€
This charming small hotel has been run by the welcoming Mansi family for years. Dotted with antiques, it has a pleasantly old-fashioned feel, and the terrace courtyard, with superb views of the sea below, is a plus. There's a restaurant; half-board is available on request.

Villa Cimbrone
Via Santa Chiara 26; tel: 089-857 144, www.villacimbrone.com; €€€€
This stunning 12th-century villa, renowned for its historic gardens, has hosted an array of famous names over the centuries, from Virginia Woolf to Bill Clinton. A 10-minute walk from Ravello's main piazza, with beautiful views at every turn, the hotel offers old-fashioned elegance rather than glamour, with traditionally styled rooms, gardens swathed in luxuriant blooms and a swimming pool with unrivalled sea views.

Capri

Capri Palace Hotel and Spa
Via Capodimonte 14, Anacapri; tel: 081-978 0111; www.capripalace.com; €€€€
Impeccable service and supremely tastefully luxurious rooms – a handful with their own swimming pools – are features of this ultra-opulent five-star clifftop retreat. Capri's choice for the rich and famous, or a serious splurge. The hotel has several restaurants, including L'Olivo, which has two Michelin stars, and Il Riccio, which has one Michelin star. Closed from November to March.

JK Capri
Via Prov. Marina Grande 225; tel: 081-838 4001; www.jkcapri.com; €€€€
When Capri's narrow streets are crammed with day-trippers, retreat to this five-star bolthole, whose breezy, vaguely nautical decor is enlivened with quirky antiques and perfumed with the scent of freshly cut blooms. With four-posters in the rooms, balconies suspended over the sea and spectacular views, waking up here is a

The clifftop pool at Palazzo Avino

treat. And you'll have almost as much fun hanging out on the huge wrap-around terrace, lounging by the infinity pool or being pampered in the spa.

La Tosca

Via Dalmazio Birago 5; tel: 081-837 0989; www.latoscahotel.com; €

With just 11 rooms, this family-run one-star place a five-minute walk from the Piazzetta is a real find in Capri – early booking is a must. Among the spotless white rooms, no. 47 is the best, with its own sunny terrace offering lovely views over San Giacomo and the hillside. All rooms have air-conditioning and Wi-fi – a bonus in this price bracket. The management is very helpful, too.

Villa Sarah

Via Tiberio 3/A; tel: 081-837 7817; www.villasarahcapri.com; €€€

A good-value relaxing hotel in a tranquil setting, a 10-minute walk from the Piazzetta. The 20 rooms have balconies facing onto well-tended grounds, and breakfast is served on a pleasant garden terrace. There's a lovely pool, which is open from May to mid-October.

Ischia

Albergo della Regina Isabella

Piazza Santa Restituta 1, Lacco Ameno; tel: 081-994 322; www.reginaisabella.com; €€€€

One of the island's most upscale choices, the Regina Isabella is glamorous, but far from snooty: perfectly coiffed *signore* are happy to be seen in their dressing gowns

at breakfast, and the staff are endlessly helpful and welcoming. Some of the rooms have been given a modern makeover, but most are classic and old-fashioned – and some are very large. The spa is highly regarded, but is more for targeted therapies than indulgent pampering; the restaurant is excellent. Check the website for bargain low-season deals.

Il Moresco

Via E. Gianturco 16, Ischia Porto; tel: 081-981 355; www.ilmoresco.it; €€

In the centre of Ischia Porto and just steps from its own private beach, this hotel is an excellent base for exploring Ischia. The decor is quite traditional in feel, and a certain old-world charm pervades: you can have aperitifs in the piano bar before moving through to the restaurant, where the dapper waiters are a paragon of old-fashioned service. The on-site spa has three pools and a raft of treatments. Half-board is usual in high season – and as the restaurant is excellent, this is no hardship.

Procida

La Casa Sul Mare

Via Salita Castello 13; tel: 081-896 8799; www.lacasasulmare.it; €€

Procida's top choice is this enchanting hotel, set in a lovely 18th-century *palazzo*. Rooms are bright and simply furnished in aquatic shades, with balconies overlooking the sea and the picture-perfect fishing village of Corricella below.

A fish restaurant in Amalfi

RESTAURANTS

In Naples the best fish restaurants and more up-market establishments with bay views are found in the Borgo Marinaro area, and in Santa Lucia, Mergellina and further west in Posillipo. For family-run trattorias, authentic pizzerias and cheaper food in general, head for the *centro storico*, where the exuberant atmosphere makes any meal memorable – even if it's just a slice of takeaway pizza.

In the more touristic coastal resorts, as a general rule restaurants in the main piazza or on the waterfront will be more expensive; for a more authentic experience, head off the tourist trail.

Eating out is central to Italian culture, and a slap-up dinner on Saturday or lunch on Sunday is a time-honoured ritual; in view of this, booking ahead is always a good idea, particularly in high season.

Restaurants generally open for business at around 12.30pm, but Neapolitans don't tend to eat until around an hour later; in the evening, restaurants open at around 7.30pm to cater to tour-

ists, but the locals are generally still quaffing *aperitivi* at that hour, heading from bar to restaurant at about 9pm. Many restaurants in Naples are closed on Sunday.

Naples

Al Faretto

Via Marechiaro 127, Posillipo, tel: 081-575 0130, www.alfaretto.com; lunch and dinner, daily; €€€

You need to make a little effort to get here as this is out on the north end of the bay in Posillipo. However, with fabulous fresh seafood, classic Neapolitan specialities and magnificent views thrown in, it's worth the effort.

Amici Miei

Via Monte di Dio 77–8, Chiaia, tel: 081-764 6063, www.ristoranteamicimiei.com; lunch and dinner Tue–Sat, Sun lunch only; closed July–Aug €€€

Small, dark and intimate restaurant, long loved for its meat specialities and classic pastas. This being Naples, fresh seafood is given its fair share of attentive preparation: no one leaves disappointed, especially after sampling the homemade fruit tarts.

Antica Latteria

Vico Alabardieri 30; tel: 081-012 8775; www.anticalatteria.it; Mon–Sat 12.30–3.30pm, 7.30pm–midnight; €€

Two-course meal for one with a glass of house wine:
€€€€ = over €40
€€€ = €26–40
€€ = €16–25
€ = under €15

Just off lively Piazza dei Martiri, this bustling, cheerful place takes its name from its origins as a dairy, and the simple, *osteria*-style decor and wood-beamed ceiling retain the old-fashioned feel. The honestly priced dishes are excellent value in this part of town: a succulent *tagliata* steak on a bed of rocket will set you back around €12.

La Chiacchierata

Piazetta Matilde Serao 37; tel: 081-411 465; Mon–Wed lunch, Thu–Sat lunch and dinner; Closed Sun and Aug; €€

A tiny family-run trattoria, La Chiacchierata – 'the chatterbox' – is one of the best places to have a meal in the historic centre. Neapolitan specialities are naturally the staples, such as tender polpette (octopus) and hearty bean-based soups. Reservations are recommended.

Ciro a Santa Brigida

Via Santa Brigida 71, tel: 081-552 4072, www.ciroasantabrigida.it; lunch and dinner Mon–Sat; €€€

Since opening in 1932, this has been an institution for regulars including Toscanini and Pirandello. Off the store-lined Via Toledo, the two-storey restaurant is always busy. Offers pizzas or a lengthy menu of classic Neapolitan dishes served by friendly house-proud waiters.

Da Michele

Via Cesare Sersale 1-7; tel: 081-553 9204; www.damichele.net; Mon–Sat 11am–11pm; €

In business for over 140 years and still going strong, this venerable pizzeria only serves two types of pizza – the classic *margherita* and the *marinara* (with a topping of tomato, garlic, oregano and olive oil) – but they are king-size and near-perfect. The decor is minimalist in the extreme – simple marble-topped tables and a vast pizza oven take up most of the space – but it has a legion of fans. Be prepared to queue.

Don Salvatore

Via Mergellina 4a; tel: 081-681817; lunch and dinner daily; www.donsalvatore.it; €€€

This lively and elegant modern restaurant is popular for its good food and seafront location (large bay window at the front opens onto the port). Specialities include a buffet of antipasti and delicious fresh fish.

Fantasia Gelati

Piazza Vanvitelli 22; tel: 081-578 8383; daily 7am–1am; €

There are always hordes of people devouring ice creams on the pavement outside this excellent *gelateria* in Vomero's lively main piazza, and a permanent queue inside – which at least gives you time to choose which of the 50-plus flavours to go for.

Friggitoria Vomero

Via Cimarosa 44; tel: 081-578 3130; Mon–

Inside Naples' Caffè Gambrinus

Sat 9.30am–2.30pm and 5–10pm; €

This Vomero institution is a great place for lunch on the run, offering fried specialities such as slices of battered aubergine, incredibly good value at just €0.20. There are sweet treats too – try the *graffe*, sugar-coated Neapolitan doughnuts. Its takeaway only – enjoy your picnic in the tranquil Villa Floridiana, a short stroll away.

Il Gobbetto

Vico Sergente Maggiore 8; tel: 081-251 2435; Tue–Sat lunch and dinner, Sun lunch only. €

Tucked away in the Quartieri Spagnoli district, this is an utterly authentic Italian trattoria, with traditional dishes (though no pizza) at very low prices. The pasta dishes are excellent, thanks to the freshness of the ingredients, and the sea bream baked in salt is a standout *secondo*. Booking essential.

Gran Caffè La Caffettiera

Piazza dei Martiri 26; tel: 081-764 4243; www.grancaffelacaffettiera.com; Mon–Thu 7am–10.30pm, Fri–Sat 7am–midnight, Sun 8am–11pm; €

This local favourite, in Chiaia's main square, is busy throughout the day: Gucci-clad *signorine* perch on the high bar stools to sip a morning *macchiato*, office suits pop in for a *panino* or a sugar-dusted pastry, and a dressed-up evening crowd gossips over *aperitivi* on the decked terrace.

La Locanda del Grifo

Via F. Del Giudice 14; tel: 081-557 1492; www.lalocandadelgrifo.com; daily noon–4pm, 7pm–midnight; €

This pizzeria-restaurant enjoys an atmospheric location, with outdoor tables on a pretty *centro storico* square just off hectic Via dei Tribunali. The huge pizzas are the draw here, but the menu also offers a handful of mainly fish-based *secondi*. Look out for the griffin that gives the restaurant its name, perched on the campanile opposite.

Mimi alla Ferrovia

Via Alfonso d'Aragona 21; tel: 081-553 8525; www.mimiallaferrovia.it; Mon–Sat noon–4.30pm, 7pm–midnight; €€

In business for 70 years and still a bastion of old-fashioned service, this traditional trattoria is an unlikely survivor in the culinary wasteland around the central station – great if you have a train to catch. Downstairs is buzzy at lunch, while the more elegant first floor is more atmospheric at dinner.

Napoli Mia

Riviera di Chiaia 269; tel: 081-552 2266; www.ristorantenapolimia.it; Tue–Sun 1–3pm, 7.30–11pm; €€€

If you need a change from Naples' ubiquitous pizzerias, head for this creative restaurant where the menu's anything but traditional: dishes might include octopus with lavender or squid-ink gnocchi with citrus and ginger. A fam-

A Gambrinus cappuccino   *Al fresco dinner in Naples*

ily affair – chef Antonella is the creative force in the kitchen, while husband Corrado is the enthusiastic front of house – the restaurant offers excellent value for cooking of this calibre.

Osteria Da Carmela
Via Conte di Ruvo 11–12; tel: 081-549 9738; www.osteriadacarmela.it; daily noon–3pm, 7–11.45pm; €€
A meal at this homely one-room *osteria*, with doily-covered tables and family paintings on the walls, feels somewhat like dinner at your elderly aunt's house. The menu is equally lacking in pretension, with a handful of simple *primi* and *secondi*. It's cheaper at lunch, with mains at just €5. A bonus is the in-house art gallery, promoting works of emerging artists.

Palazzo Petrucci Pizzeria
Piazza San Domenico Maggiore 4 I, 80134, tel: 081-551 2460, www.palazzopetrucci. it; closed much of August, daily noon–11.30pm; €€–€€€
Definitely one of the best pizzerias in town. Efficient service and reasonable prices (pizzas start at €5) make the Palazzo Petrucci a great pit stop, set in an amazing 17th-century palazzo.

La Scialuppa
Borgo Marinaro 4; tel: 081-764 5333; www.ristorantelascialuppa.it; Tue–Sun 12.30–3pm, 7.30–midnight; €€€
Bag a table on the flower-filled terrace or soak up the atmosphere in the dining room, with huge windows overlooking the Borgo Marinaro. Fish is the speciality, but you can order a pizza and enjoy the same views for a fraction of the price.

Un SorRiso Integrale
Vico S. Pietro a Maiella 6; tel: 081-455 026; www.sorrisointegrale.com; daily 12.30–4pm, 7pm–11.30pm; €€
The perfect antidote to pizza and pasta overload, this organic vegetarian restaurant-cum-health food store is in a small courtyard off Piazza Bellini. With fresh flowers on communal wooden tables and crates of fresh produce dotted around, it has an appealingly homespun feel, and the food's good, too: big salads, soups, cheese plates and home-made cakes. The *piatto unico*, a selection of the day's specials, costs €9.

Taverna dell'Arte
Rampe S. Giovanni Maggiore 1A; tel: 081-552 7558; Mon–Sat 7.30–11pm; €€–€€€
Hidden away on a side street near Via Mezzocannone, this is many people's idea of the perfect little Italian trattoria: terracotta-tiled floors, walls lined with wine bottles and simple white linen on the tables; four tables sit under a flower-strewn bower outside. Simple, well-executed dishes include meatballs with local greens and home-made soups (no pizza).

The Borgo Marinaro has restaurants aplenty

Campi Flegrei

Grottino a'Mmare

Via dell'Emporio 15, Pozzuoli; tel: 081-526 2480; daily 10am–4pm and 6–midnight, closed Mon in winter; €€€

A smart choice, with simple, elegant table settings on a decked terrace overlooking the water, this place has been serving up the freshest of the day's catch since 1912; the *pezzogna* fish is the one to go for.

Pompeii

Il Principe

Piazza Bartolo Longo 8; tel: 081-850 5566; www.ilprincipe.com; €€€

If you haven't packed a picnic for Pompeii and fancy a splurge, this prestigious restaurant is the place. The regional dishes are excellent, but the special menu of contemporary dishes inspired by ancient Roman recipes is what really sets it apart. You need to call first to request this, but the speciality *cassata di Oplontis*, a delectable ricotta cheesecake sweetened with honey and studded with candied fruits, is always on the menu.

Sorrento and the Peninsula

Il Buco

Rampa Marina Piccola 2a, Sorrento; tel: 081-878 2354; www.ilbucoristorante.it; Thu–Tue 12.30–2.30pm, 7.30–11pm; €€€€

Don't be fooled by the name ('The Hole'): this swanky, Michelin-starred establishment is Sorrento's top restaurant, serving up dishes such as

pork medallions in a prune sauce with crispy onions and asparagus. Tasting menus range from €55 for three courses to €100 for an eight-course feast (plus €50 for wine to complement the meal). Eat in the ancient brick-arched dining room or outside on stepped terraces. The restaurant is tucked into the stone vaults of the Basilica di Sant'Antonino.

La Conca del Sogno

Via Amerigo Vespucci 25, Nerano; tel: 081-808 1036; www.concadelsogno.it; €€€

Finding this tucked-away restaurant is not easy, but worth the effort. As you drive down towards Marine del Cantone, after Nerano follow signs to the Villaggio Syrenuse. Ask for permission to drive through this campsite, beyond which the road cuts through a ravine and opens out on to a tiny beach and the lovely Conca del Sogno – an excellent restaurant that also has six rooms. Call if you want their shuttle boat to pick you up from Marina del Cantone.

Da Franco

Corso Italia 265, Sorrento; tel: 081-877 2066; daily noon–2am; €

This rowdy locals' pizzeria is at Corso Italia's non-touristic end. Take a seat at one of the communal wooden tables and watch your pizza being prepared by one of the expert *pizzaioli* in the open kitchen. The house special

Capri café

is topped with tomato, cheese, rocket and parmesan, but there are plenty of other options to tempt you, too.

Don Alfonso 1890

Corso Sant'Agata 11–13, nr Sorrento; tel: 081-878 0026; www.donalfonso.com; closed Mon-Tue, Nov–Mar; €€€€

Pilgrims of gastronomy know the 7km (4.5-mile) drive from Sorrento to the hills 365m (1,200ft) above sea level is a price willingly paid for a meal at one of Italy's finest and most renowned restaurants, the proud holder of two Michelin stars. Superchef Alfonso Iaccarino uses produce from his farm to create the culinary masterpieces his family's long-established restaurant is renowned for. The award-winning wine cellar is one of the largest and best in Italy (and that's saying something). The dining room is suitably elegant – all Murano glass and hand-painted majolica – and tasting menus range from €140 to €155. Book well in advance. There are rooms, if you wish to stay, and a cookery school.

La Fenice

Via degli Aranci 11, Sorrento; tel: 081-878 1652; www.ristorantelafenice.org; €€€

This restaurant/pizzeria is attractively decorated and has a welcoming atmosphere. Seafood and antipasti are the specialities, on a menu that has something for all budgets.

Sant'Antonino

Via Santa Maria delle Grazie 6, Sorrento;

tel: 081-877 1200; daily noon–11.45pm; €€

Right in the centre of Sorrento but tucked away in an elevated position up a flight of steps, this restaurant is a hit with locals and tourists alike for its delicious food and jovial service. There are no bay views, but dining on a terrace full of citrus trees makes up for it; look out for the hybrid that grows both oranges and lemons.

Taverna del Capitano

Piazza delle Sirene 10–11, Marina del Cantone; tel: 081-808 1028; www.tavernadelcapitano.com; Tue-Sun 12.30–2.30pm, 7.30–10pm; closed mid-Jan to mid-Mar and Tue in winter; €€€€

Marina del Cantone is renowned for its fish restaurants, and this is one of the best. With two Michelin stars and a stellar reputation, it invites high expectations, and the superb fish dishes don't disappoint. The dining room is lined with inlaid wood, and the wine cellar, set in the cherry-wood hull of a reproduction Sorrentine ship, is fabulous.

Amalfi

Da Gemma

Via Fra Gerardo Sasso 11; tel: 089-871 345; www.trattoriadagemma.com; Thu–Tue noon–3pm, 7–11pm; €€€€

This landmark trattoria, in business since 1872, is famous for its fish

Lunch in Amalfi

soup and its surprisingly delicious aubergine-and-chocolate dessert, but there are many standout dishes: try the catch of the day baked in a salt crust, or the citrus-marinated tuna carpaccio. Whether you eat inside in the spacious, airy dining room or on the elegant roof terrace with views of the Duomo, booking is essential.

Dolceria dell'Antico Porto

Supportico Rua; tel: 089-871 143; Tue–Sun 8.30am–9pm; €

This boutique *pasticceria* in the heart of Amalfi is an essential stop for foodies. The owner, Tiziano Mita, is a whiz with pastry, taking the long-established Neapolitan tradition to new heights; his *sfogliatella* is given a new twist in the shape of a *trullo* – the typical Puglian conical-roofed house – while the traditional *delizia* lemon-cream cake is paired with an olive-oil biscuit. Melt-in-the-mouth lemon and almond pastries are another speciality.

Ravello

Cumpà Cosimo

Via Roma 44–46; tel: 089-857 156; daily noon–3pm, 7–11pm; €€€

Family-run since opening in 1929, this one-room trattoria may look homely but it has hosted a galaxy of celebrity diners over the years, from Jackie Onassis to Mariah Carey. The cooking is simple but delicious: you might have ham and figs to start, followed by grilled prawns, rounded off with home-made cheesecake.

Rossellinis

Palazzo Avino, Via San Giovanni del Toro 28; tel: 089-818 181; www.palazzoavino.com/en/Dining/Rossellinis; Apr–Oct 7.30–9pm; €€€€

In the opulent surroundings of the Hotel Palazzo Avino, this two-Michelin-starred restaurant has a splendid setting, its terrace perched high above the bobbing lights of the fishing boats below. A highlight of the tasting menu is lamb fillet in a rose crust with white asparagus, in an anchovy and sun-dried tomato sauce.

Villa Maria

Via Santa Chiara 2, tel: 089-857255; www.villamaria.it; daily for lunch and dinner; winter closures vary; €€€

Relaxed yet refined, this is one of the prettiest settings for lunch with a bird's-eye panorama, or for dinner with a high romance quotient. Classical music drifts through the pergola-covered alfresco terrace and cosy indoor dining room of this century-old villa that also offers a dozen rooms. The chef knows his regional specialities, beginning with the homemade spaghetti-like scialatielli that are typical of Naples.

Positano and environs

Buca di Bacco

Via Rampa Teglia 8; tel: 089-875699;

Fresh clams

You won't go short of pasta in Naples

www.bucadibacco.it; daily for lunch and dinner, closed Nov–mid-Mar; €€€

Together with Chez Black, this second-storey arbor-covered restaurant is one of the most enduring of the beachfront see-and-be-seen scenes. Its best main courses are the simply grilled fresh fish. Book early for the railing-side tables with a view of the action below. A pre-dinner drink at the first-floor open-sided bar is de rigueur.

Chez Black

Via del Brigantino 19; tel: 089-875036; www.chezblack.it; daily 11am–midnight Mar–early Jan; €€€

A stylish, fashionable restaurant that is one of a cluster snuggled directly on the beach. It offers very good-quality food and value-for-money considering its prime location and long-time popularity. For an informal lunch or relaxed dinner, it's one of the better choices in town for great pizzas and pastas, with reliably fresh fish for more serious dining.

Da Vincenzo

Viale Pasitea 172–178; tel: 089-875 128; Mar–Oct daily 12.30–3pm, 7–11pm, closed Tue lunch end June–Oct; €€€

This family-run restaurant is not the cheapest in town, but worth the splurge for the outstanding cooking and local delicacies that you'll only find here: a typical starter might be *totani e patate* – squid cooked with potatoes – followed by a main of sea bream flavoured with lemon and orange peel and baked in a bread crust. Neapolitan music in the evening adds to the buzzy atmosphere.

Donna Rosa

Via Montepertuso 97–99, Montepertuso; tel: 089-811 806; www.drpositano.com; Wed–Mon 11am–3pm, 6–10pm, Aug dinner only; €€€€

Just above Positano, the quieter, more workaday village of Montepertuso harbours several very good restaurants, but Donna Rosa is the standout choice, and is packed with dressed-up locals every night. The expertly prepared seafood is the main draw, although the stunning views come a close second. Leave room for dessert – the hot chocolate soufflé is to die for. The restaurant will pick you up from Positano at a set time, or it's a €20 taxi ride. Booking essential.

Capri

Aurora

Via Fuorlovado 18, Capri; tel: 081-837 0181; www.auroracapri.com; daily noon–3pm, 7pm–midnight; €€€€

This is one of Capri's smartest restaurants, with dishes such as fish carpaccio with vanilla salt and pine nuts, and linguine with lobster and asparagus, though (pricey) pizzas are on offer, too. The elegant terrace dotted with pots of fragrant blooms is right on

Pizza is the Naples staple

Capri's main shopping strip, making it prime people-watching territory – but booking for dinner rather than lunch will make for a more tranquil experience.

Canzone del Mare

Via Marina Piccola 93; tel: 081-837 0104; www.lacanzonedelmare.com; €€€€

In the former home of English singer Gracie Fields, this resort hotel embedded in the rocks was a jet-set destination in its heyday, and remains a little reminiscent of the 1960s. The location of the terrace restaurant remains as stunning as ever, beside a swimming pool surrounded by gardens with views of the Faraglioni, and the food is of good quality, if expensive. Open daily 9am–7pm. Suites also available, if you want to splash out and stay. The names, meaning 'Song of the Sea', refers to the hauntingly beautiful singing of the sirens, who lured sailors to their death on the rocks.

Da Alberto

Via Roma 9–11; tel: 081-837 0622; www.pasticcerialberto.com; daily 5.30am–midnight, Nov–Mar closed Tue, Aug open 24 hours; €

In business since 1946, Da Alberto is a good spot for a coffee and a wedge of *torta caprese* – Capri's deliciously moist almond-and-chocolate namesake. In August, the bar is famous for its *cornetto caldi* (hot-from-the-oven croissants), served all night long to bleary-eyed bar-hoppers.

Da Paolino

Via Palazzo a Mare 11, Marina Grande; tel: 081-837 6102; www.paolinocapri.com; Apr–Oct, dinner only in April–May; €€€€

You may find yourself fighting Hollywood A-listers for a table at one of Italy's most romantic restaurants, where the candlelit tables, piled high with mouth-watering antipasto, are set amidst the lemon groves. Save up for a splurge and book well ahead.

La Pigna

Via la Palazzo 30; tel: 081-837 0280; www.caprigourmet.it; €€€

With gorgeous views over the Gulf of Naples, this elegant restaurant is the perfect place for a romantic dinner, especially if you can get a table on the terrace. The food, which is served with flair, combines local and international influences.

Pulalli

Piazza Umberto 4; tel: 081-837 4108; Wed–Mon noon–3pm, 7pm–midnight, Aug open daily; €€€

Wonderfully sited in the bell tower overlooking the Piazzetta, this elegant restaurant and wine bar is reasonably priced (for Capri). *Scialatielli verdi* (pasta with prawns and rocket) is the house speciality, and the walls are lined with over 300 wines. Book to be sure of a table on the terrace.

Lunch in Ischia

Local lemons

Terrazza Brunella

Via Tragara 24; tel: 081-837 0122; www.terrazzabrunella.com; Easter to Oct daily noon–3pm, 7–11pm; €€€€

Near Punta Tragara, a 10–15 minute walk from the Piazzetta, is this atmospheric restaurant, with a spectacular clifftop perch offering breathtaking views – booking a table by the window is a must. The food is excellent: try the lobster linguine or the king prawns with cognac.

Ischia

Calise Caffè Concerto

Piazza degli Eroi, Ischia Porto; tel: 081-991 270; daily 6am–2am; €–€€

An Ischian institution, this vast place is a bar, *pasticceria* and pizzeria in one, and even a club in the summer months, with live music nightly. Its lushly planted gardens make a great place for an *aperitivo*, and if the chattering crowds get too much, there are plenty of little hidden corners to retreat to.

Da 'Peppina' di Renato

Via Montecorvo 42, Località Forio; tel: 081-998312; www.trattoriadapeppina.it; €€€

Furnished with old barrels, this enticing *trattoria* offers local cuisine, such as pasta mischiata (pasta with beans, lentils or chickpeas) and homemade crostate (tarts). Reservations are essential.

Neptunus

Via lo Russo 1, Forio d'Ischia; tel: 081-904 255; www.ristoranteneptunus.com; €€€

Perched on a cliff and enjoying spectacular views, this colourful restaurant has a vibrant atmosphere in the evenings, when there's live musical entertainment. Its fresh-off-the-boat fish, expertly prepared, attracts the great and the good and photographs of VIP visitors are proudly displayed.

Umberto a Mare

Via Soccorso 2, Forio; tel: 081-997 171; www.umbertoamare.it; daily noon–11pm, closed Nov–Mar; €€€€

This upscale restaurant offers panoramic views and superb but pricey fish dishes. At lunch, you can feast on dishes such as linguine with tuna, capers and olives for €12. There's also an elegant café.

Procida

La Conchiglia

Chiaia beach; tel: 081-896 7602; www.laconchigliaristorante.com; daily 9am–midnight; €€

Right on Chiaia beach, La Conchiglia is a wonderful place for a family lunch (this is one of the safer beaches for children) or a romantic dinner, with views to swoon over. Pasta with mussels and courgettes is a speciality *primo*, and the grilled fish is superb. No road access; take a taxi boat from Corricella or walk down the steps from Via Pizzaco.

Family fun on a moped

A–Z

A

Age restrictions

The age of consent in Italy is 14. In order to drive legally in Italy you must have your full UK licence and be at least 18 years of age. There is no minimum drinking age, but you have to be over 16 to be served drinks in a public place.

B

Budgeting

Naples is inexpensive, though prices soar in resorts along the Amalfi Coast and on Capri. The following is a general guide to give you an idea of how to budget.

Food and drink

A glass of house wine in Naples will cost €1.50, on Capri €4; a beer is €3 in Naples, €5 in Capri. At an inexpensive trattoria, main courses go for €5–8; in moderate places, €10–15; in expensive restaurants €18–25.

Hotel prices

Hotel rates vary hugely, but a double room in a cheap hotel in Naples will cost €50–90; a moderate hotel €90–150; in low season, deluxe rooms are as little as €150, though in high season the sky's the limit: the fanciest places on the Amalfi Coast and islands will set you back upwards of €600.

Transport costs

Public transport is cheap: a 90-minute ticket within Naples is €1.50, or a weekend day from Naples to Sorrento just €4.50 (valid for 180 minutes). Hydrofoils are pricier: around €16 one-way from Naples to Capri, though slower ferries and the Metrò del Mare summer services are a little cheaper.

Entrance charges

The major museums and archaeological sites charge from €4 to €17. Most state-run museums and sites offer free entrance to EU citizens under 18 or over 65, with a lesser discount to those aged between 18 and 25. Many state museums offer free entrance on the first Sunday of each month. Entrance to most churches is free.

Campania Artecard

If you are planning to see quite a few sights during your trip, the **Campania Artecard** (www.artecard.it) could be a worthwhile investment. Several varieties are available; one particularly useful option is the Napoli Card, which gives free access to the first three of the many key attractions in Naples, plus half-price entry on all remaining sights, and includes public transport (valid for

Naples' Palazzo Reale

A busy beach in Ischia

three days; €21). The three-day Tutta la Regione card (€32) includes even more sights, including Campi Flegrei and Pompeii. Buy the card online, at participating museums, at tourist offices or from the Artecard info-point in the central station.

C

Children

Feeding children in Naples and along the coast (and indeed in the rest of Italy) isn't usually a problem, since most kids – of all ages – like pasta and pizza. Most find the ice creams delicious too. Neapolitans, like all Italians, are very fond of children (over-indulgent if anything), and big family meals are the norm in restaurants, so you are unlikely to encounter any problems. Of course, it's up to you to ensure that your children behave well and don't disturb other customers.

Disposable nappies (diapers) and baby food and formula milk are as easy to buy in Italy as in most of Europe and the US. You often get a wider selection in pharmacies than in supermarkets.

Nappy-changing facilities are not widely available, although you will usually find them in more upmarket restaurants and, if you are driving, at motorway service-station toilets.

Bring your own pushchair and baby carrier, as you are unlikely to find them for hire. However, child seats are usu-

ally available as extra items when hiring a car.

Child-friendly sights and attractions

In terms of places to take children, the Villa Comunale has plenty of space for kids to let off steam, as well as an aquarium, and the Parco di Capodimonte is a good place to kick a ball around.

Older children might enjoy a visit to Pompeii or Herculaneum – especially if it's preceded by a virtual-reality reconstruction – or the intriguing underground sights of Napoli Sotterranea and the catacombs, or the geological wonders of Vesuvius and the Solfatara.

The Città della Scienza (Via Coroglio 104; tel: 081 7352 220/222; www.cittadellascienza.it; Tue–Sat 9am–3pm, Sun 10am–5pm) is part of the redevelopment programme of the old Bagnoli steelworks. In March 2017 a brand new 3D Planetarium with 120 seats and CORPOREA, the first human body museum in Europe, will be opened to the public. The hi-tech hands-on science park is a fun day out for children and adults; take bus R7 from Naples' Piazza Vittoria.

Hiring a boat in Sorrento, the Amalfi Coast or the islands and pottering between beaches can be a fun way to spend a day.

And if all else fails, take the kids to the thoroughly revamped **Edenlandia** (Viale Kennedy 76, Fuorigrotta; tel: 081-239 4090; www.edenlandia.it), a tradi-

A romantic moment in Naples

tional theme park just outside Naples. Take the Cumana train from Montesanto to get there.

Clothing

Light summer clothes are suitable from spring to autumn. The heat is sometimes alleviated by a sea breeze by day and evenings can be cool, even in summer, so keep a jacket on hand. Hats and sunglasses are recommended for sun protection.

Rainfall is rare in mid-summer, but when the deluge does come, it's often a surprise afternoon shower that rarely lasts for a long time. November to January is notoriously rainy, so bring your raincoat. In winter, you'll want to dress in layers.

Crime and safety

Despite its reputation as a hotbed of crime, Naples is no more dangerous than any other big European city, if you take the usual precautions. The main problem tourists experience is pickpocketing and bag-snatching, together with theft from parked cars.

Wear bags across the body if possible and be wary of nimble-fingered lads whizzing by on mopeds. Be especially vigilant on crowded buses and around Piazza Garibaldi, the Quartieri Spagnoli and La Sanità.

Report a theft *(furto)* as soon as possible; you will need to go to the police to make a statement *(denuncia)*. The police report will be required for any insurance claim and to replace stolen documents.

For information on the nearest police station, call Naples' Questura Centrale, near Piazza Municipio at Via Medina 75, tel: 081-794 1111, or ask for the *questura più vicino*.

Customs

Visitors from EU countries are not obliged to declare goods imported into or exported from Italy if they are for personal use, up to the following limits: 800 cigarettes, 200 cigars or 1kg of tobacco; 10 litres of spirits (over 22 percent alcohol) or 20 litres of fortified wine (under 22 percent alcohol).

For US citizens, the duty-free allowance is 200 cigarettes, 50 cigars; 1 litre of spirits or 2 litres of wine; one 50g bottle of perfume and duty-free gifts to the value of US$200–800, depending on how often you travel.

Disabled travellers

Central Naples is not an easy place for people with disabilities. However, things are improving, with ramps and lifts being installed in museums, stations and hotels. Capri's hotels in particular are good at meeting individual needs, and as there are no steps, it can be easier to get around, though the slopes are steep and buses are not wheelchair-accessible. An accessible route at Pompeii makes naviga-

Sunset on the Amalfi Coast

Enjoying the evening sunshine

tion of the site easier for those with reduced mobility.

Call 199 303 060 for assistance on trains, and 848 888 777 for help at the airport.

The website www.accessibleitaly.com is useful for pre-trip planning, and www.turismoaccessibile.it is another excellent resource, with detailed information on accessible museums, restaurants and hotels.

Electricity

Standard is 220 volts. Sockets are generally two round pins.

For UK visitors, adaptors can be bought before you leave home, or at airports and stations. Travellers from the US will need a transformer.

Embassies and consulates

If your passport is lost or stolen, you will need to obtain a police report and have proof of your identity to get a new one. Many countries have embassies in Rome, but several have consulates in Naples.

Australia: 5 Via Antonio Bosio, Rome; tel: 06-852 721; www.italy.embassy.gov.au

Canada: 30 Via Zara, Rome; tel: 06-854 441; www.canadainternational.gc.ca/italy-italie

Ireland: Villa Spada, Via Giacomo Medici, Rome; tel: 06-585 2381; www.dfa.ie/irish-embassy/italy/

New Zealand: 44 Via Clitunno, Rome; tel: 06-853 7501; www.mfat.govt.nz

UK: 80a Via XX Settembre, Rome; tel: 06-4220 0001; www.gov.uk

US: Piazza della Repubblica, Naples; tel: 081-5838 111; https://it.usembassy.gov

Emergency numbers

National emergency number, including police and medical emergencies: tel: 113

Carabinieri: tel: 112
Ambulance: tel: 118
Fire: tel: 115

Gay/lesbian travellers

Attitudes towards gay relationships in Naples and the main resorts are reasonably tolerant, though smaller towns may be more conservative. The national organisation Arcigay has a branch at Vico San Geronimo alle Monache 19, off Via Benedetto Croce; tel: 081-5528 815; www.arcigaynapoli.org. It offers information and advice, and organises events for the local gay community.

For general information on the scene in Italy, see www.gay.it.

Health

In theory, EU and Australian citizens are entitled to reciprocal care (visitors will need to obtain an EHIC card, www.

Piazza Plebiscito in Naples

ehic.org.uk, before they go; Australians are covered by Medicare). Nonetheless, it's a good idea to take out travel insurance.

The standard of care is generally high, though the state of hospitals themselves may not inspire confidence.

US citizens are not covered under Italian law, so will need to take out private health insurance.

Chemists

Chemists *(farmacie)* have a large green cross on the outside. The pharmacy at Napoli Centrale station is open 7am–10pm; *Il Mattino* newspaper carries details of late-night pharmacies. For more information, and listings, visit www.farmaciediturno.net.

Emergencies

If you need emergency treatment, call 118 for an ambulance or information on the nearest hospital with an emergency department *(pronto soccorso)*.

Hospitals

Naples' most central hospitals with *pronto soccorso* (emergency) departments are in Vomero: Cardarelli at 9 Via Cardarelli; tel: 081-747 1111 and Santobono (for children under 12) at 6 Via Mario Fiore; tel: 081-220 5734.

Hours and holidays

In general, shops open Mon–Sat 9am–1pm and 4–7pm or 8pm, although the bigger ones now stay open later, and even open on Sundays. Most restaurants close on Sundays. Many shops and restaurants close for at least two weeks in August. Banks generally open Mon–Fri 8.30am–1.30pm and 2.45–4pm. Some branches may also be open on Saturday mornings.

Opening times of churches and museums vary enormously and change twice a year, with a longer timetable for summer (Easter–Oct) and a shorter one for winter (Nov–Easter). Most churches open early in the morning but close at around noon or 12.30pm until 3pm or 4pm, closing again in the evening between 7pm and 8pm; some open in the morning only.

Many museums are closed on Monday and ticket offices close one hour before the official closing time. Archaeological sites close one hour before sunset; two hours in the case of Pompeii and Herculaneum.

The times given in this guide are as accurate as possible, but may be subject to change. If in doubt, check with the tourist office or online.

Most businesses are closed on the following public holidays:
New Year's Day (1 January)
Epiphany (6 January)
Easter Monday (date varies)
Liberation Day (25 April)
Labour Day (1 May)
Founding of the Republic (2 June)
Assumption of the Virgin Mary (15 August)
Feast of San Gennaro (Naples only, 19

Posing in Pompeii

September)
All Saints' Day (1 November)
Immaculate Conception (8 December)
Christmas Day (25 December)
St Stephen's Day (26 December)

Internet facilities

For free Wi-fi hotspots in Naples check www.wifisharing.co/italy/free-wifi-na ples. All major hotels, shopping malls, post offices and cafes in Naples offer Wi-fi. Internet cafés cluster around the station. Expect to pay around €2–4 for an hour's internet access.

Money

Currency

The unit of currency in Italy is the euro (€), which is divided into 100 cents. There are 5, 10, 20, 50, 100, 200 and 500 euro notes, coins worth €1 and €2, and 1, 2, 5, 10, 20 and 50 cent coins.

Credit and debit cards

Major credit cards are accepted by most hotels, shops and restaurants, though some smaller places remain cash-only. Cash machines (ATMs), called Banco-mat, can be found throughout central Naples and the main resorts, and are the easiest and generally the cheapest way of obtaining cash; in smaller towns ATMs are scarcer.

Changing money

You need your passport or identification card when changing money. Not all banks will provide cash against a credit card, and some may refuse to cash traveller's cheques in certain currencies. On the whole, exchange bureaux *(cambio)* outside of touristic areas offer better rates than banks. Traveller's cheques are the safest way to carry money around, but not the most economical since banks charge a large commission for cashing them.

Tipping

Most hotel prices are quoted as all-inclusive *(tutto compreso)*, meaning the service charge is included. Many restaurants impose a cover and bread charge *(coperto and pane)*, although officially it has been eliminated. Often, a 10–15 per cent service charge *(servizio)* is added to the bill; if not, it is usual to leave 10–15 per cent. Hotel porters, maids and door-men, bartenders, toilet attendants and service-station attendants expect a tip of €1–2. For taxi drivers, round the fare up to the nearest euro. If you have a tour guide, a tip is expected, but how much you give depends on the service you receive and the size of your party.

Post

Post offices are open Mon–Fri 8am–1.30pm or until 6.30pm (large branches), Sat 8am–12.30pm; the main post office

Market fish stall

in Naples is at 2 Piazza Matteotti (Mon–Fri 8am–6.30pm, Sat 8am–12.30pm).

Italian postboxes are usually red with two slots, *per la città* (for the city) and *tutte le altre destinazioni* (everywhere else).

Stamps *(francobolli)* can be bought at many tobacconists *(tabacchi)* – look for the sign with the white letter 'T' on a black background. For fast delivery (up to three days in Europe and five to the rest of the world), ask for *posta prioritaria* (priority post) stamps.

Smoking

Smoking is banned in all public spaces in Italy, except in those establishments that have created a specially ventilated smoking area, though this is rare.

T

Telephones

Dialling codes and useful numbers
The prefix for Italy is +39. The local code is 081.

When calling abroad from Italy, first dial 00 (the international access code), then the country code (44 for the UK; 353 for the Republic of Ireland; 1 for the US and Canada; 61 for Australia; 64 for New Zealand), the area code and then the subscriber number.

For international directory enquiries, tel: 176; for reversed-charge (collect) calls, tel: 170.

Directory enquiries: 12

Payphones and phone cards
Most public payphones accept phone cards *(scheda telefonica)* only. You can buy cards in various denominations from *tabacchi* and many newsstands. Some payphones accept credit cards, and some bars have coin-operated payphones. There are a number of cheap international phone cards available from newsstands, and call centres where you can make your call and pay later.

Mobile phones
Mobile (cell) phone reception is based on GSM technology, which is not compatible with US non-tri-band phones. If you have an unlockable GSM, dual- or tri-band phone, consider buying an Italian SIM card from local providers TIM, Vodafone or Wind, which cost from €10. To buy a sim you will need to present a form of identification, such as a passport or European ID card. Numbers starting with a 3 are mobile numbers and will cost more to call than landline numbers.

Time zones

Italy follows Central European Time (GMT+1). From the last Sunday in March to the last Sunday in September, clocks are advanced one hour (GMT+2).

Toilets

Bars are obliged by law to let you use their toilets. This doesn't mean that they will do so with good grace; if you don't spend any money at the bar first

Café on the Borgo Marinaro

Stunning view of the Amalfi Coast

they may throw you a look. In many cases bar toilets are locked and you will need to ask for the key *(chiave)* at the till; once inside you may find out that there is no soap or toilet paper.

Tourist information

In Italy

Naples: 7 Piazza del Gesù, tel: 081-551 2701; 9 Via San Carlo, tel: 081-402 394; there's also an infopoint at the airport. The tourist board's website, www.inaples.it, is useful.

Campi Flegrei: 3 Via Campi Flegrei, Pozzuoli, tel: 081-526 2419.

Pompeii: Piazza Porta Marina Inferiore 11, tel: 081- 850 8451.

Sorrento: 35 Via L. De Maio, tel: 081-878 2104.

Positano: 4 Via del Saracino, tel: 089-875 067.

Amalfi: 27 Corso Repubbliche Marinare, tel: 089-871 107.

Ravello: 10 Piazza Duomo, tel: 089-857 096.

Capri: 1 Piazza Umberto I, Capri Town, tel: 081-837 0686.

Ischia: 116 Corso Vittorio Colonna, tel: 081 991 464.

Procida: Via Roma, tel: 081-810 1968.

Tourist information abroad

Italian Government Tourist Board: 1 Princes Street, London W1R 8AY; tel: 020-7408 1254 www.london.enit.it.

Italian Government Tourist Board: 686 Park Ave, New York 10065; tel: 212-245 5618; www.newyork.enit.it.

Tours and guides

City Sightseeing open-top buses run on three lines in Naples and the surrounding area (www.napoli.city-sightseeing.it), all of which depart from Piazza Municipio. Tickets cost €22 and last for the day, allowing you to hop on and off as you please. Services also run in the Sorrentine Peninsula and on the Amalfi Coast; see www.sorrento.city-sightseeing.it or tel: 081-877 4707 for details. The Sorrentine bus is a good option if you want to leave the driving in route 7 to the locals – it runs from outside the station in Sorrento to Massa Lubrense, Termini and Sant'Agata sui due Golfi. The round trip takes an hour and 40 minutes. You can hop on and off, as the ticket is valid for 6 hours, but bear in mind that buses only run every two hours.

Context Travel offers small-group and private walking and car tours lead by art historians and archaeologists (tel: 06-4890 0042 or 1 800 691 6036, www.contexttravel.com). Options range from specialised Baroque walks to shopping tours; prices start at around €75 per person.

Transport

Arrival by air

Naples' airport, **Capodichino** (tel: 081-789 6111, www.aeroportodinapoli.it), is 7km (4 miles) from the city centre. The **Alibus airport bus** stops at Piazza Garibaldi train station and the

Neapolitan guards

port every 20-30 minutes and runs from Mon–Fri 6.30am–11.40pm, Sat–Sun 6.30am–11.45pm, at a cost of €4 (tel: 081-763 1111, www.anm.it). The bus leaves from outside Arrivals and takes 15–20 minutes to reach Piazza Garibaldi, 30–35 minutes to reach Piazza Municipio. Another option is the cheaper S3 bus, which is much slower as it stops frequently.

Curreri buses (www.curreriviaggi. it) run every 75 minutes to Sorrento from outside Arrivals (9am–8.45pm; €10; 1hr 15min). The same bus stops at Pompeii (same price; 25 minutes) en route.

A **taxi** to the port should cost about €19, to Piazza Garibaldi €16, to Vomero or hotels along the Lungomare near Chiaia €23. Check the list of fixed-price fares next to the tourist information desk. If you want to pay a fixed fare, you need to request it at the start of the journey (ask for *tariffa fissa*).

Arrival by rail or bus

Most trains from other parts of Italy and Europe arrive at the main station, **Napoli Centrale** (www.napoli centrale.it) in Piazza Garibaldi. Metro and suburban rail lines also pass through here, and outside is a terminus for city and long-distance buses. From Piazza Garibaldi, take bus 1 to the port area, metro line 2 to Montesanto or bus R2 for the *centro storico*, or metro line 2 to Amedeo or Mergellina for Chiaia.

Arrival by boat

Frequent hydrofoils from Sorrento, the Amalfi Coast and islands arrive at Naples' port, Molo Beverello. Some services run from the islands and Pozzuoli to the smaller port of Mergellina, connected to the city by metro line 2. Larger, slower ferries from the islands arrive at Calata Porto di Massa, a 10-minute walk east of Molo Beverello. For schedules, check daily paper *Il Mattino*, or the tourist offices.

Arrival by road

From the UK, the usual route is through France, entering Italy at the Alps and taking the autostrada down to Naples.

Public transport

The transport network within the bay area is very efficient and all the major sites and resorts are well served by buses, trains and boats. Pompeii, Herculaneum and Vesuvius are easily reached by train on the Circumvesuviana line from Sorrento or Naples. Towns in the Campi Flegrei area are served by the Naples Cumana and Circumflegrei regional metro lines (formerly the SEPSA lines). Transport connections between the islands and coastal resorts are efficient and reasonably priced. Ask at the tourist office for the free transport map.

Tickets. UnicoCampania tickets (www. unicocampania.it) are available in various different forms covering the whole region, and are sold in *tabacchi* shops.

Within Naples, you will need a UnicoN-apoli ticket, available as a 90-minute ticket €1.50, all-day pass €4.50, or a €15.80 weekly pass. Alternatively, the Artecard passes allow free travel on public transport within the covered area (the entire of Campania). There are also cheaper ANM and EAV tickets, starting at just €1.00, that cover only one journey, using only one line, with no interchanges, that are supplied by two independent companies.

On board buses, stamp your ticket in the machine; on metros, it needs to be stamped at the entrance gate.

Buses. Progress through the traffic-choked streets is often painfully slow. The main intersection is Piazza Municipio (bus stop outside the Castel Nuovo) and Via San Carlo (bus stop outside Galleria Umberto I). The most useful lines are: R1 (for the Archaeological Museum and Piazza Dante), R2 (to the train station), 140 (Riviera di Chiaia and Mergellina), R4 (Capodimonte).

SITA buses (www.sitasudtrasporti. it) have the Sorrento peninsula and Amalfi Coast covered. Buses from Sorrento to Positano and Amalfi depart in front of the main station (for Ravello you need to change at Amalfi). SEPSA buses serve the Naples suburbs and the Campi Flegrei. Two routes on Ischia circumnavigate the island; on Capri there are regular bus services between the major points of interest; buses on Procida link the port to the main villages.

Metros. The metro, currently being extended, can be very useful, especially Line 2, which stops at Piazza Garibaldi, Montesanto (for Via Toledo and connections to the Campi Flegrei), Piazza Amedeo (for Chiaia and the Vomero funicular), Mergellina and Pozzuoli. Line 1 runs between Piazza Dante, Museo (for the Archaeological Museum) and northeast Naples via Piazza Vanvitelli (Vomero); when complete, this line will be circular and link the city centre and the airport. Services operate 6am–11pm, with trains every 8–12 minutes.

Funiculars. Naples' funiculars serve the Vomero district. The Funicolare Centrale leaves from the bottom end of Via Toledo, the Funicolare di Chiaia from Piazza Amedeo and the Funicolare di Montesanto links Montesanto station to Via Morghen (nearest to the Vomero attractions). For more details, see www.anm.it.

Trains. Napoli Centrale can be a confusing place to take a train. The main train station (tel: 892 021, or 06-6847 5475 from abroad; www.napoli centrale.it) is on the ground floor; downstairs are the metro and Circumvesuviana services (for Pompeii, Herculaneum and Sorrento; tel: 081-7722 111; www.sitabus.it/circumves uviana-orari-e-tariffe). To catch a Circumvesuviana train (roughly every 30 minutes), it's best to go to the more orderly terminus at Porta Nolana, a few streets south.

The original Fiat 500

Cumana trains (www.eavsrl.it/) for the Campi Flegrei depart from Montesanto station (Metro line 2) in the centre of town.

Tickets for Trenitalia trains can be bought online or by phone, and picked up from one of the self-service machines in the station, where you can also buy your tickets directly. Buy UnicoCampania tickets for Circumvesuviana and Cumana services from the ticket office at the terminus of the line or from *tabacchi* shops. The stops along the line are divided into various fare zones; a one-way ticket to Pompeii costs €3.20 and €4.50 to Sorrento. Tickets for all trains must be stamped before boarding at one of the yellow machines.

Ferries. There are frequent crossings between Naples, the islands and Sorrento. In summer there are services to the Amalfi Coast towns, too. Hydrofoils *(aliscafi)* depart from Molo Beverello, near Castel Nuovo, the smaller port of Mergellina to the west and Pozzouli. The main operators are Caremar (tel: 081-1896 6690; www.caremar.it), Snav (tel: 081-428 55 55; www.snav.it), NLG (tel: 081-552 0763; www.navlib.it), Alilauro (tel: 081-497 2238; www.alilauro.it) and Gescab (tel: 081-704 1911; www.gescab.it). The Metrò del Mare service (tel: 199-600 700), which usually runs in summer, is cheap and frequent.

Ferries *(traghetti)* are slower, but you can sit on deck and take in the coastal scenery as you go. Caremar has the inter-island monopoly and Medmar (tel: 081-333 4411; www.medmargroup.it) runs an Ischia service. All ferries leave from Calata Porta di Massa, a 10-minute walk from Molo Beverello. There are also services to Ischia and Procida from Pozzuoli.

Taxis. Meters in white taxis tend to start at around €3.50 (€6 on holidays). Between 10pm and 7am; on Sundays; for luggage; and for airport pick-ups and drop-offs there is a surcharge. If the meter *(tassometro)* isn't switched on, point this out to the taxi driver, or agree a fixed price *(tariffa fissa)* before starting. You can order a radio taxi by phone (tel: 081-556 4444 or 081-8888) for a supplement of around €1. Don't worry too much about tipping; most drivers will do the rounding up for you. Water taxis also operate in the coastal resorts and island ports.

Driving

Unless you want to venture off the beaten track and explore the hinterland, driving is not a sensible option for getting around: the traffic is horrendous (particularly along the Amalfi Coast in summer), parking is a problem, and if you're not used to driving in Italian cities, the general disregard for the rules of the road will do little for your stress levels.

If you're determined to drive, note that Naples' *centro storico* is off-limits to non-residential vehicles at certain

Ferry at Procida   *A fully loaded scooter*

times of the day (look for the ZTL – *zona a traffico limitato* – signs), and that you cannot take a car on to Capri.

Car and scooter rental. You can rent a car at the airport, though it's a good idea to book before you arrive. Rates are usually inclusive of insurance, but check to make sure you're completely covered. Most rental companies will supply a car with a full tank.

The following companies have outlets at the airport:

Avis (tel: 081-780 5790; www.avisauto noleggio.it)

Europcar (tel: 081-780 5643; www. europcar.it)

Hertz (tel: 081-780 2971; www.hertz.it)

Maggiore (tel: 081-780 3011; www. maggiore.it)

Sixt (tel: 081-751 2055; www.sixt. com).

Renting a scooter is to be avoided in Naples, but can be a fun way of getting around the islands; on Ischia, the largest island, you may be better off with a car. In the Amalfi Coast area, try Positano Rent A Scooter (tel: 089-812 2077; www.positanorentascooter.it).

Parking. Street parking costs €2–€5, though in Naples supervised parking is a must. Parking lots *(parcheggio)* are marked with a blue 'P'. The most convenient is at the port, Molo Beverello (tel: 335-499 658; www. parcheggiobeverello.com; open 24 hours a day). You can also park along the blue lines in the city centre area (Mon–Sat); although rates are steep

and start at €2 for the first hour, and €0.50 for the next. One-hour parking on Sundays and holidays is slightly cheaper, costing €1 for two hours.

Outside Naples, make sure your hotel has parking facilities; Positano has several car parks in the upper town, but parking restrictions in Ravello and Amalfi mean you have to leave your car outside town.

Petrol. Petrol stations *(benzinaio)* are usually manned – just ask *il pieno*, which means 'fill her up'. Rates vacillate around €1.50 a litre. For unleaded ask for *senza piombo*. Some stations accept credit cards, but it's a good idea to carry cash in case they don't.

Visas and passports

EU passport-holders do not need a visa; a valid passport or ID card is sufficient. Visitors from the US, Canada, Australia and New Zealand do not require visas for stays of up to three months; non-EU citizens need a full passport.

Nationals of most other countries, including South Africa, do need a visa. This must be obtained in advance from the Italian Consulate.

Free exchange of non-duty-free goods for personal use is allowed between EU countries. Nationals of other countries should refer to their home country's regulating organisation for a list of import restrictions.

Newspaper kiosk

LANGUAGE

Italian is relatively easy to pick up, if you have any knowledge of French or Spanish (or a grounding in Latin). Most hotels have staff who speak some English, and unless you go well off the beaten track, you should have little problem communicating in shops or restaurants. However, there are places not on the tourist circuit where you will have the chance to practise your Italian, and local people will think more of you for making an effort. Here are a few basics to help you get started.

Useful phrases

General
Yes *Sì*
No *No*
Thank you *Grazie*
Many thanks *Mille grazie/Tante grazie*
You're welcome *Prego*
All right/That's fine *Va bene*
Please *Per favore/Per cortesia*
Excuse me (to get attention) *Scusi*
Excuse me (in a crowd) *Permesso*
Could you help me? (formal) *Potrebbe aiutarmi?*
Certainly *Ma, certo/Certamente*
Can you show me...? *Può indicarmi...?*
Can you help me, please? *Può aiutarmi, per cortesia?*
I need... *Ho bisogno di...*
I'm lost *Mi sono perso*
I'm sorry *Mi dispiace*

I don't know *Non lo so*
I don't understand *Non capisco*
Do you speak English/French/Spanish? *Parla inglese/francese/spagnolo?*
Could you speak more slowly? *Può parlare più lentamente, per favore?*
Could you repeat that please? *Può ripetere, per piacere?*
How much does it cost? *quanto costa?*
this one/that one *questo/quello*
Have you got...? *Avete...?*

At a bar/restaurant
I'd like to book a table *Vorrei prenotare un tavolo*
Have you got a table for... *Avete un tavolo per...*
I have a reservation *Ho prenotato*
lunch/supper *il pranzo/la cena*
I'm a vegetarian *Sono vegetariano/a*
May we have the menu? *Ci dia la carta?*
What would you like? *Che cosa prende?*
I'd like... *Vorrei...*
mineral water fizzy/still *acqua minerale gasata/naturale*
a bottle of *una bottiglia di*
a glass of *un bicchieri di*
red/white wine *vino rosso/bianco*
beer *una birra*

Numbers
One *uno*
Two *due*
Three *tre*
Four *quattro*

Sgraffito　　　　　　　　　　　　*Hand gestures are also important*

Five *cinque*
Six *sei*
Seven *sette*
Eight *otto*
Nine *nove*
Ten *dieci*
Twenty *venti*
Thirty *trenta*
Forty *quaranta*
Fifty *cinquanta*
One hundred *cento*
One thousand *mille*

Getting around
What time do you open/close? *A che ora apre/chiude?*
Closed for the holidays *Chiuso per ferie*
Where can I buy tickets? *Dove posso fare i biglietti?*
What time does the train leave? *A che ora parte il treno?*
Can you tell me where to get off? *Mi può dire dove devo scendere?*
Where is the nearest bank/hotel? *Dov'è la banca/l'albergo più vicino?*
On the right *a destra*
On the left *a sinistra*
Go straight on *Va sempre diritto*

Online
Where's an internet cafe? *Dov'è un Internet caffè?*
Does it have wireless internet? *C'è il wireless?*
What is the WiFi password? *Qual è la password Wi-Fi?*
Is the WiFi free? *Il WiFi è gratis?*

How do I turn the computer on/off? *Come si accende/spegne il computer?*
Can I...? *Posso...?*
access the internet *collegarmi (a Internet)*
check e-mail *controllare le e-mail*
print *stampare*
plug in/charge my laptop/iPhone/iPad? *collegare/ricaricare il mio portatile/iPhone/iPad?*
access Skype? *usare Skype?*
How much per hour/half hour? *Quanto costa per un'ora/mezz'ora?*
How do I...? *Come...?*
connect/disconnect *ci si collega/scollega*
log on/log off *si fa il login/logout*
What's your e-mail? *Qual è la sua e-mail?*
My e-mail is... *La mia e-mail è...*

Social media
Are you on Facebook/Twitter? *È su Facebook/Twitter? (polite form) Sei su Facebook/Twitter? (informal form)*
What's your user name? *Qual è il suo nome utente? (polite form) Qual è il tuo nome utente? (informal form)*
I'll add you as a friend. *La aggiungerò come amico. (polite form) Ti aggiungerò come amico. (informal form)*
I'll follow you on Twitter. *La seguirò su Twitter. (polite form) Ti seguirò su Twitter. (informal form)*
I'll put the pictures on Facebook/Twitter. *Metterò le foto su Facebook/Twitter.*
I'll tag you in the pictures. *La taggherò nelle foto.*

A scene from the film Gomorrah

BOOKS AND FILM

A dazzled Goethe, visiting Naples in 1786, declared that "one may write or paint as much as one likes, but this place, the shore, the gulf, Vesuvius, the citadels, the villas, everything, defies description. Now I can forgive anyone for going off his head about Naples". The unique charms of Naples and the Amalfi Coast have long inspired creative types, awe-struck Grand Tourists and modern-day cinematographers alike. Naples' unabashed exuberance has lured a legion of writers, from Charles Dickens to Graham Greene, while the vibrant colours, intense light and a stunning natural tableau of rugged mountains, sea and sky make the region effortlessly film-worthy.

The list of books below makes a good starting point for some background reading before your trip, while the recommended films portray the region and its development over the last half-century, from a sun-drenched Capri in the carefree '60s to the grim mafia-run suburbs of present-day Naples.

Books

The Ancient Shore, Shirley Hazzard. An eloquent love letter to Naples, by an American writer who lived in the city for decades. This book collects Hazzard's best writings, interspersing them with evocative photographs.

Capri and No Longer Capri, Raffaele La Capria. A nostalgic portrait of Capri from the time of Homer to the present day.

Cosi Fan Tutti, Michael Dibdin. In the fifth book of the popular Aurelio Zen detective series, Zen is putting Naples and its shady criminal underworld to rights. A sparkling holiday read.

Falling Palace, Dan Hofstadter. A powerful homage to the author's beloved Naples, "that beautiful and wounded city", and the local woman who captivated him. The colourful character studies of the author's Neapolitan friends are priceless.

Greene on Capri, Shirley Hazzard. For more than 40 years, Graham Greene spent part of the year at his villa in Anacapri. Hazzard's evocative memoir stems from her long friendship with the elusive writer, and provides an intriguing glimpse both into his life and into a bygone Capri.

My Brilliant Friend, Elena Ferrante. A gripping story of two childhood friends, Elena and Lila, who grow up together in the outskirts of Napoli during the 1950s. As they grow older, their paths repeatedly cross. It is also a tale of a changing neighbourhood, city and country, by one of the most popular modern Italian writers.

Naples '44, Norman Lewis. Lewis' memoir of his time as an intelligence officer in a war-torn Naples is a fascinating and often harrowing account of a city on the verge of collapse, and its people surviving on their wits. A must-read.

A scene from Passione

Pompeii, Robert Harris. A pacey thriller that brings that fateful day in 79 AD to life. Harris' masterful recreation of everyday life in ancient Italy makes an enjoyably explosive read.

In the Shadow of Vesuvius, Jordan Lancaster. Exploring three thousand years of Naples' history, and touching on art, literature, cuisine, music, film and popular culture, this book provides a useful and readable overview.

The Story of San Michele, Axel Munthe. The heartwarming story of Munthe, a Swedish doctor, and his discovery and restoration of a crumbling villa on Capri, the Villa San Michele – now one of the island's biggest draws.

The Volcano Lover, Susan Sontag. Set in eighteenth-century Naples, Sontag's celebrated historical romance portrays the famous love triangle between Sir William Hamilton, his wife, Emma, and her lover, Lord Nelson.

Film

Gomorrah (2008). Unsettling film adaptation of Roberto Saviano's novel of the same title, providing a chilling exposé of Naples' most infamous criminal organisation, the Camorra. The film was produced by Matteo Garrone, who used the city's run-down suburbs as a set and cast untrained locals as actors

Gomorrah TV series (2014-16). Also based on Roberto Saviano's novel, this critically acclaimed production resembles *The Wire*, providing a fascinating insight into mafia hierarchy and internal power struggles, from the perspective of both the foot soldier, and the *capo di tutti capi* (boss of all bosses).

L'Oro di Napoli (1954). Naples-born comic genius Totò joins Sophia Loren in this collection of six vignettes set in Naples.

Marriage Italian Style (1964). Vittorio de Sica's romantic comedy, featuring both Sophia Loren and Marcello Mastroianni, which launched the pair into international stardom.

Passione (2010). This documentary by actor-turned-director John Turturro is a passionate tribute to Naples' songs and singers.

Il Postino (1994). Chilean poet Pablo Neruda is exiled to a small island in Italy and strikes up a friendship with the local postman. A heartwarming tale, filmed on a sun-drenched Procida.

Sciuscià (1947). A classic of Neorealist cinema by Vittorio de Sica, this moving film deals with the scugnizzi, Neapolitan street children, at the end of World War II.

It Started in Naples (1960). Fluffy romantic comedy starring Sophia Loren and Clark Gable, who fall in love on Capri.

The Talented Mr Ripley (1999). The much-loved dramatization of Patricia Highsmith's psychological thriller makes good use of Ischia and Procida's old-world charm.

Voyage to Italy (1954). Roberto Rossellini cast his wife Ingrid Bergman in this poignant tale of a marriage falling apart against the backdrop of Pompeii, Capri and Naples.

ABOUT THIS BOOK

This *Explore Guide* has been produced by the editors of Insight Guides, whose books have set the standard for visual travel guides since 1970. With top-quality photography and authoritative recommendations, these guidebooks bring you the very best routes and itineraries in the world's most exciting destinations.

BEST ROUTES

The routes in the book provide something to suit all budgets, tastes and trip lengths. As well as covering the destination's many classic attractions, the itineraries track lesser-known sights, and there are also ex-cursions for those who want to extend their visit outside the city. The routes embrace a range of interests, so whether you are an art fan, a gourmet, a history buff or have kids to entertain, you will find an option to suit.

We recommend reading the whole of a route before setting out. This should help you to familiarise yourself with it and enable you to plan where to stop for refreshments – options are shown in the 'Food and Drink' box at the end of each tour.

For our pick of the tours by theme, consult Recommended Routes for… (see pages 6–7).

INTRODUCTION

The routes are set in context by this introductory section, giving an overview of the destination to set the scene, plus background information on food and drink, shopping and more, while a succinct history timeline highlights the key events over the centuries.

DIRECTORY

Also supporting the routes is a Directory chapter, with a clearly organised A–Z of practical information, our pick of where to stay while you are there and select restaurant listings; these eateries complement the more low-key cafés and restaurants that feature within the routes and are intended to offer a wider choice for evening dining. Also included here are some nightlife listings, plus a handy language guide and our recommendations for books and films about the destination.

ABOUT THE AUTHORS

Natasha Foges moved to Italy in 2003 for one year and ended up staying for four, during which time she took on an array of jobs, from paparazzo's assistant to Latin teacher, before trying her hand at travel journalism. Now an editor and travel writer based in London, she spends much of her time pining for the southern Italian sunshine, and goes back as often as she can to soak up the atmosphere and tuck into some world-class pizza. Many of the tours in this book were originally conceived by Italy expert Cathy Muscat. Thanks also go to Clare Peel.

CONTACT THE EDITORS

We hope you find this Explore Guide useful, interesting and a pleasure to read. If you have any questions or feedback on the text, pictures or maps, please do let us know. If you have noticed any errors or outdated facts, or have suggestions for places to include on the routes, we would be delighted to hear from you. Please drop us an email at hello@insightguides.com. Thanks!

CREDITS

Explore Naples and the Amalfi Coast
Editor: Tom Fleming
Author: Natasha Foges
Head of Production: Rebeka Davies
Update Production: AM Services
Picture Editor: Tom Smyth
Cartography: original cartography Berndston & Berndston GmbH, updated by Carte
Photo credits: Alamy 27L, 36, 67, 74/75; Corbis 49L; Getty Images 4/5T, 8/9T, 22, 23, 25L; Greg Gladman/Apa Publications 4ML, 4MC, 4MR, 4MR, 4MC, 4ML, 6TL, 6MC, 6ML, 6BC, 6T, 7MR, 7M, 8ML, 8MC, 8ML, 8MC, 8MR, 8MR, 10, 10/11, 11L, 12/13, 14, 14/15, 15L, 16, 16/17, 18, 18/19, 19L, 20, 20/21, 21L, 24, 24/25, 26, 28ML, 28MC, 28MR, 28ML, 28MC, 28MR, 28/29T, 30, 30/31, 32, 32/33, 33L, 34, 34/35, 35L, 36/37, 38, 38/39, 40, 40/41, 41L, 42, 42/43, 43L, 44, 44/45, 45L, 46/47, 48/49, 50, 50/51, 52, 52/53, 54, 54/55, 55L, 56, 56/57, 58, 58/59, 59L, 62, 62/63, 63L, 64, 64/65, 65L, 66, 68/69, 70, 70/71, 72, 72/73, 73L, 74, 75L, 76, 77L, 76/77, 78, 79L, 78/79, 80, 80/81, 82, 82/83, 83L, 84/85, 86MR, 86MC, 86MC, 96, 96/97, 98, 98/99, 99L, 100, 100/101, 102, 102/103, 103L, 104, 104/105, 105L, 106, 106/107, 107L, 108, 108/109, 109L, 110, 110/111, 112, 112/113, 113L, 114, 114/115, 116, 116/117, 117L, 118, 118/119, 119L; iStock 1, 7MR, 60, 61, 86MR; Leonardo 86ML, 88, 88/89, 89L, 90, 91, 92, 92/93, 93L, 94; Mary Evans Picture Library 26/27; Moviestore/REX/Shutterstock 120; Palazzo Avino 86ML, 86/87T, 95; Scala 48; Skydancers/REX/Shutterstoc 121
Cover credits: Shutterstock (main&bottom)

Printed by CTPS — China

Second Edition 2017

Every effort has been made to provide accurate information in this publication, but changes are inevitable. The publisher cannot be responsible for any resulting loss, inconvenience or injury.

DISTRIBUTION

UK, Ireland and Europe
Apa Publications (UK) Ltd
sales@insightguides.com
United States and Canada
Ingram Publisher Services
ips@ingramcontent.com
Australia and New Zealand
Woodslane
info@woodslane.com.au
Southeast Asia
Apa Publications (Singapore) Pte
singaporeoffice@insightguides.com
Hong Kong, Taiwan and China
Apa Publications (HK) Ltd
hongkongoffice@insightguides.com
Worldwide
Apa Publications (UK) Ltd
sales@insightguides.com

SPECIAL SALES, CONTENT LICENSING AND COPUBLISHING

Insight Guides can be purchased in bulk quantities at discounted prices. We can create special editions, personalised jackets and corporate imprints tailored to your needs.
sales@insightguides.com
www.insightguides.biz

INDEX

MAP LEGEND

● Start of tour

— Tour & route direction

❶ Recommended sight

❷ Recommended
    restaurant/café

Ⓜ Metro station

★ Place of interest

ⓘ Tourist information

♁ Statue/monument

✉ Main post office

🚌 Main bus station

🏠 Villa

•┄•⛟ Cable car

⁂ Ancient site

🏰 🏚 Castle / ruin

🜨 Cave

Park

Important building

Hotel

Transport hub

Shop / market

Pedestrian area

Urban area

INSIGHT ◎ GUIDES
OFF THE SHELF

Since 1970, **INSIGHT GUIDES** has provided a unique perspective on the world's best travel destinations by using specially commissioned photography and illuminating text written by local authors.

Whether you're planning a city break, a walking tour or the journey of a lifetime, our superb range of guidebooks and phrasebooks will inspire you to discover more about your chosen destination.

INSIGHT GUIDES

offer a unique combination of stunning photos, absorbing narrative and detailed maps, providing all the inspiration and information you need.

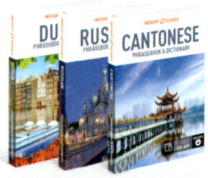

PHRASEBOOKS & DICTIONARIES

help users to feel at home, when away. Pocket-sized with a free app to download, they go where you do.

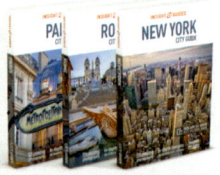

CITY GUIDES

pack hundreds of great photos into a smaller format with detailed practical information, so you can navigate the world's top cities with confidence.

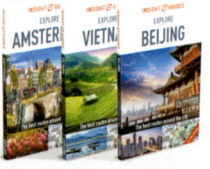

EXPLORE GUIDES

feature easy-to-follow walks and itineraries in the world's most exciting destinations, with our choice of the best places to eat and drink along the way.

POCKET GUIDES

combine concise information on where to go and what to do in a handy compact format, ideal on the ground. Includes a full-colour, fold-out map.

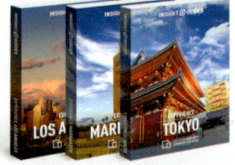

EXPERIENCE GUIDES

feature offbeat perspectives and secret gems for experienced travellers, with a collection of over 100 ideas for a memorable stay in a city.

www.insightguides.com

INSIGHT ⊙ GUIDES

EXPLORE

NAPLES

 # Walking Eye App

Your guide now includes a free eBook to your chosen destination, for the same great price as before. Simply download the Walking Eye App from the App Store or Google Play to access your free eBook.

HOW THE WALKING EYE APP WORKS

Through the Walking Eye App, you can purchase a range of eBooks and destination content. However, when you buy this book, you can download the corresponding eBook for free. Just see below in the grey panel where to find your free content and then scan the QR code at the bottom of this page.

Destinations: Download essential destination content featuring recommended sights and attractions, restaurants, hotels and an A–Z of practical information, all available for purchase.

Ships: Interested in ship reviews? Find independent reviews of river and ocean ships in this section, all available for purchase.

eBooks: You can download your free accompanying digital version of this guide here. You will also find a whole range of other eBooks, all available for purchase.

Free access to travel-related blog articles about different destinations, updated on a daily basis.

EXPLORE

HONG KONG

荔枝角
Lai Chi Kok